Trish ~

May you always
feel God giving you
and showering you
with His grace

and love.

Kari B. Pollock

Growing Up Gracefully

KAREN B. POLLOCK

CROSSBOOKS
PUBLISHING

CrossBooks™
A Division of LifeWay
1663 Liberty Drive
Bloomington, IN 47403
www.crossbooks.com
Phone: 1-866-879-0502

First published by CrossBooks 6/15/2012

ISBN: 978-1-4627-1883-2 (sc)
ISBN: 978-1-4627-1901-3 (hc)
ISBN: 978-1-4627-1884-9 (e)

Library of Congress Control Number: 2012909526

Printed in the United States of America

This book is printed on acid-free paper.

Any people depicted in stock imagery provided by Thinkstock are models, and such images are being used for illustrative purposes only.

Certain stock imagery © Thinkstock.

Because of the dynamic nature of the Internet, any web addresses or links contained in this book may have changed since publication and may no longer be valid. The views expressed in this work are solely those of the author and do not necessarily reflect the views of the publisher, and the publisher hereby disclaims any responsibility for them.

Table of Contents

For my parents—
Kenny and Edna
who provided my first vision of God through their
sacrificial love and tender nurturing

and to my three sisters—
Laura, Angela, and Mendy
who have grown up with me and been
constant companions in the adventures of this life

Foreword

Written by Darrin J. Pollock

Ordinary is a word that drives us. It drives us away from that which makes our lives—or even more terrifying, ourselves—*traditional, typical, commonplace, undistinguishable, mediocre*. We fixate on the notion that we must stand out from among the crowd; for our worth and acceptance, our secular culture (and to some extent, our contemporary Christian culture) will suggest, depends on our ability to outshine others. But sadly, *ordinary* does not glisten.

So we run from *ordinary*. We analyze every *ordinary* part of our lives—our background, education, appearance, job, family, house—and loathe it. Fanning the flames of dissatisfaction of the *ordinary*, we secretly envy the "super-Christians"—the Billy and Franklin Grahams, the Charles Stanleys, the Joyce Meyers, the Popes, the numerous contemporary Christian musician-preachers, the self-sacrificing missionaries, the virtual saints in our own churches—whose righteousness casts a profound shadow over our *ordinary*. We admire their walk with God because it seems so exceptional, so stellar, while ours—just *ordinary*. Upon a pedestal (or more accurately an altar), we lift these "super-Christians" above our *ordinary* and revere them and mimic them and envy them and praise them, for they must be more holy, more significant, more loved. And once again, we loathe our *ordinary*. For how can God be satisfied with us—just *ordinary*?

But what we fail to understand is that God embraces *ordinary*. Throughout the Bible, from Jael to Hannah to David to Elijah to Esther to Joseph to Mary, the mother of Jesus—the list goes on—God uses seemingly *ordinary* people to fulfill His purposes. To accomplish His tasks and to simply commune with Him, God does choose those with prestige and power; yet according to the Bible, time and time again, He selects the poor, the weak, the insignificant, the discounted, the rejected, the *ordinary*. Did God not take an *ordinary* tribe of *ordinary* men and *ordinary* women to create the consecrated nation of Israel? Did He not select an *ordinary* family to raise His Son and twelve *ordinary* men to become His disciples? Did His Son not teach *ordinary* people through parables composed of *ordinary* subjects? God delights in the *ordinary*.

Karen B. Pollock's devotional *Growing Up Gracefully* challenges us to reconsider our mindset about *ordinary*. Through stories of her life, she sifts through the seemingly *ordinary* moments and extracts the gold therein that God has used to inspire and transform her. The devotional reflects on subjects most of us encounter in our *ordinary* lives; however, through her insightful musings, Karen B. Pollock empowers the *ordinary* and reveals how God uses such moments to transform our lives into a more reflective, fulfilling, and intimate journey with Him.

In *Growing Up Gracefully*, underlying questions continuously whisper, waiting to be answered: "What if you began to accept, despite what some in our culture (and even the contemporary Christian culture) regard as, your *ordinary* life? What if you stopped comparing the lives God ordained for others to the life God ordained for you?"

As we read the devotional and reflect, how might we respond? Would we finally live the "abundant life" by embracing our weaknesses along with our strengths? Would we finally appreciate our *ordinary* daily struggles along with the blessings? Would we finally find peace in every moment of our *ordinary* lives? Would we finally allow God to delight in our *ordinary*?

Karen B. Pollock challenges us to follow her in examining our *ordinary* lives, experiences, and the Word of God to commune with Him. And then, the distraction and envy that blinds us, gradually melts away to reveal a paradox: when we accept that which in us is *ordinary*, only then can we see that which in God and His work is truly *extraordinary*.

Acknowledgments

Heartfelt thanks to Stephen for believing in me every step of the way, supporting me in more ways than one, and for F&A. Eric and Ray for keeping me on my toes and teaching me to laugh at myself. Kaitlin Rae, Madilyn Grace, Elizabeth Grace, and Emma Kate for making my world more beautiful, carefree, and unique. Ethan Lamar, Brody Beckham, Samuel Jake, and Nate Robert for contagious laughter, bear hugs, and secret snuggles.

Special thanks to Hariette for instilling the power of prayer in me and reigniting my desire to write. Marie for being the first to trust me to share my gift of words with students.

The Willow Tree

Written By: Stephen J. Holbrook

The willow tree
It is often forgotten
Never spoken highly of
Yet It withstands the test
of time
Over and over again
It is much like us
In more ways than not
As each day comes
It stands there prepared for
what's to come
It doesn't back down
It simply just stands there
in wait
Its branches grow and blossom
It begins to show Its colors
The weeping branches sway
In a way that leaves me
to wonder
What stories would It tell if It
could only speak
In time It grows old
But never really weakens
It has become hard on Its
outside shell
With Its knowledge, It looks as
if It has much sorrow

However towards the end
It is left standing
It has learned to trust Its roots
To take what It was given
To offer shade to many
To live without regret

The willow tree
The One that is often
forgotten
But never forgets you
And doesn't turn Its back
Rather It invites you to gather
Under Its limbs
To offer protection from what's
at hand

The willow tree
The One that bears no
judgment
The One that takes me for me
It is the only One
That stands beside me
In my weakest of moments
In my times of sorrow
The good times and the bad
Forever It stands

Keeper of the Willows

"Blessed is the man who trusts in the LORD and
whose trust is in the Lord. For he will be like a
tree planted by the water that extends its roots by a
stream . . ." Jeremiah 17:7–8a (NASB)

Trees are one of God's most wondrous creations; especially the
weeping willow tree. Typically, they stand alone—isolated from
the company of other trees. They require no companionship aside
from the adoring humans that seek refuge in their shade. Their
conversation consists of whispers with the wind and their touch
is the occasional tickling of the grass that lies beneath it. It is easy
to look at the willow and conclude that it believes in something
greater than itself. The vibrant green branches bow as if worshipping
its Creator and the sheer majesty of the willow is disguised with
humility. As a child, I longed to have a weeping willow tree in the
yard. We were blessed with towering oaks and regal dogwoods, but

not a single weeping willow. I dreamt of building an imaginary world up under its branches. I would tiptoe in the shadows and become the princess of a magical kingdom. I would marry my knight in shining armor and cradle my babies in the branches of the weeping willow.

A few years ago, I decided to take matters into my own hands. I went to the nursery and purchased a weeping willow tree. I chose the perfect spot in my yard, dug a hole, filled it with water, and plopped the tree into the ground. Each day throughout the spring and summer, I carried a five gallon bucket of water to the tree and drenched it. Even on rainy days, I gave my tree a fresh drink of water. I made sure that the roots were protected with loose soil and fresh mulch. Every day felt like Arbor Day and I was proud to be giving back to nature.

However, I noticed in late July that the tree wasn't growing. The willow was barely taller than me and that wasn't saying much at all. The only changes I did notice were yellowing leaves and peeling bark—not indicators of a flourishing tree. I began to feel discouraged as my little tree deteriorated. What in the world had I done wrong? I had given my heart and soul to nurture the willow. I boasted and told myself, "*You are the keeper of the willow and you know best.*" I frantically marked off my checklist: *rich soil, tender loving care, sunshine, gentle touch, w—a—t—e—r.*

When I finally let go of my pride and consulted an expert, I learned that I had chosen an inappropriate spot to plant my tree. He said that the willow needed to be placed in an area where the roots could grow toward a natural water source. I also discovered that I had drowned my tree. Although weeping willows need their fair share of water, there is a better way for them to get it than a shocking shower from a bucket. I had meant well, and I thought I could nurture the tree into the dream I had built up in my mind. I had dared to do the work of the roots and failed. I never stopped to consider that the tree possessed an ability to prosper in its own special way—drawing strength from its intricate root system.

As I think about the things I need in life to grow and mature, I realize that God has equipped me in such a way that I can become something magnificent and wonderful for Him. God desires that I grow in His grace and knowledge. He longs to set me apart and use me as His vessel. I may be called to do difficult things—impossible things; however, He becomes my All in All so that He might be glorified through me. His love stretches the roots of my heart and I draw upon His strength and nourishment. My Lord is constant, trustworthy, and dependable. My time here on earth is a like a vapor, but He uses every moment to establish my life story. And whether those moments are frustrating or fabulous, His enduring love allows me to continue *growing up gracefully*.

Myrtle Mae Sees the Light

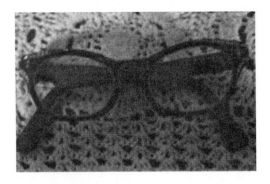

I started wearing glasses when I was in 5th grade. I spent months squinting and lying to my parents about my poor eyesight. I certainly didn't want to get glasses and be labeled as *"four eyes"* or *"nerd."* Finally, when I could stand it no longer, I broke down and told my mom that I couldn't see things that were distant. We went to the eye doctor and I cried my eyes out through the entire visit.

The only thing I liked about the visit was getting to choose a pair of glasses. Although I dreaded the prospect of being called names, I was completely smitten with accessorizing with cool glasses. My first pair of frames was large and perfectly round. The stylish choice was to add a sticker decal to the bottom right corner of the lens—I chose a beautiful butterfly. From that moment on, I had a true obsession with glasses. Right now, I have five different pairs that I rotate depending upon my mood. My favorite is a pair of authentic cat eyes that I purchased in a vintage store.

It didn't take me too long to realize that wearing glasses not only allowed me to make a statement, but they enlightened my world. I was seeing through new eyes and my improved eyesight changed my life. The fuzzy, chaotic vision I had grown accustomed to was now crisp and clear. I took notice of things that had once been a haze to me. I was crazy and stubborn to live with unhealthy vision when there was a perfectly wonderful solution to my problem.

Sometimes, I allow the eyes of my heart to become blurred by selfish ambition . . . uninspired motivation . . . irrational fear. Terror destroys my life as I wander in the darkness—snatched up in Satan's scheme to set me on a path of aimless destruction. I grow so cold and desperate that I forget how to find my way back to God. I know that I need His touch, but I just can't see clearly. I find myself in tears; terrified of being ridiculed by the world.

It is a ridiculous individual who will grope in the darkness when they can simply place their trust in the God of heaven and earth and find a light that passes all human understanding. As with my physical vision, my spiritual vision can be corrected. God wants to be the power that opens the eyes of my heart. He wants the scope of my vision to be focused and unhindered.

"God is light and in Him there is no darkness at all."
I John 1:5 (NASB)

Because of God's promises and love for me, I no longer have to be trapped in a black hole of turmoil. I have been buried with Him in death and raised to walk in the newness of life. People can insult me and even call me names, but I am triumphant and can experience all of the beauty of life because His brilliance pours over me:

"The LORD is my light and my salvation; whom shall
I fear? The LORD is the defense of my life; of whom
shall I dread?" Psalm 27:1 (NASB)

Just for the record, I was never called a name because of my glasses until very recently. I wore my vintage glasses to church and a young guy said, "You know who you look like?" Suddenly my wind was twirling to figure out what celebrity I must remind him of. He finally said, "Myrtle Mae! Remember? Steve Urkel's cousin." After 32 years, my worst fear had surfaced and all I could do was laugh. I laughed because there was a little bit of truth in what the guy had said.

A Horse Named Silver and the Holy Spirit

I wasn't much on cowboys, guns, and horses when I was a little kid. However, I did enjoy watching *The Lone Ranger* with my dad. The mask, the Indian, the horse that could speed like a bullet . . . these things captured my attention. I knew that this masked man *stood* for something and *believed* in something.

The goal these days is to seek change. We want everything to be new and improved. When change and improvement happens, our lives become faster paced and appear to become easier. Companies will change anything to make an extra buck. As if a Milky Way wasn't already good enough, they went and added mint to the candy bar. They took a perfectly delicious M&M and put a pretzel inside. In their effort to make radical changes, I tend to scramble for something that is sure, steady, reliable, and stable. One statement in the Lone Ranger's Creed is: *All things change, but the truth, and the truth alone lives on forever.*

Indeed, the Lone Ranger was driven and determined to know and uphold the truth. He stood for something and his way of dealing with things proved that he was forever seeking truth. My truth is God's Word.

> "All Scripture is inspired by God and profitable for
> teaching, for reproof, for correction, for training in
> righteousness." II Timothy 3:16 (NASB)

I have a firm grasp on a Truth that surpasses all logic and reason. It is a Truth that covers my temptation—my anxiety—my fear—my pain. It is a Truth that looks beyond my fault and sees my need. It is a Truth that rejoices with me and weeps with me. It is a Truth that dwells within me and is demonstrated in my life. What is hidden in my heart cannot be snatched away.

As we muddle through our daily lives trying to fulfill our mission, we find ourselves in situations not so different than the Lone Ranger. We are called on to represent integrity and honor. People expect us to live up to certain expectations. We have to make decisions that are not always popular from the world's perspective. Often, we wonder exactly how we are supposed to gracefully take care of all the priorities in our life. Another statement in the Lone Ranger's Creed is: Everyone has within himself the power to make this a better world.

The Lone Ranger drew his power from a deep desire to seek justice. He relied on his best friend, Tonto to be committed and dedicated to the cause. His other strengths were his mysterious identity, his gun, and the famous horse, Silver. There was never a doubt that the Lone Ranger would make everything okay in the end.

I have within me the power to face each new day with joy and determination. Yes, God has called me to do specific ministries, to love people, to serve, and to live a life set apart from the world. This power comes through the promise declared in the Word.

"But you will receive power when the Holy Spirit has
come upon you ..." Acts 1:8 (NASB)

The Holy Spirit does not come with a mysterious mask, a shiny
gun, or a sleek stallion. It doesn't even come with the promise of
complete resolution at the end of a conflict. However, it does bring
protection, peace of mind, and a perseverance to fight evil for the
common good. In fact, I can be a Lone Ranger of the faith.

A Lifetime

"Pray without ceasing." I Thessalonians 5:17 (NASB)

It amazes me that the God of the universe wants me to talk to Him. He draws me near and allows me to rest in His goodness, compassion, and mercy. It is during these intimate encounters that I sense God's presence in my life the most. I approach my conversations with God trusting that He will answer my prayers . . . *quickly!* I love it when the answer is immediate and obvious. He gives me those moments to appreciate his sweet, swift Spirit. Naturally, I conclude that I was faithful to pray, God was faithful to answer, and I can faithfully move to my next request lickety-split.

I've heard stories where people petitioned God with the same request for extraordinarily long periods of time. So long, in fact, that they may have appeared foolish to those around them. I have often wondered if their groaning resembled the incessant buzzing of a bumblebee in God's ears. Even in the Bible, there were individuals who undoubtedly grew weary of bowing and rising, bowing and rising, bowing and rising with the same prayer day after day. In I Samuel I, Hannah expresses her deep longing for a child. She literally prayed for years with no results. Just when she had met her point of desperation, Hannah paused, pondered on the longing of her heart, and . . . prayed *again*. This woman truly cherished the promise "with God nothing is impossible." Hannah obviously believed that her God could answer her prayer. Otherwise, she would have gone cold on the whole idea of prayer before she had the chance to see His glorious answer revealed.

For nearly a year, one prayer has echoed from my heart. Not a single day passes that I don't speak to Him at depth about my desire. I consider the petition honorable. If He chose to answer my prayer, I believe I would grow as an individual and believer. Were God to answer the prayer, it would be uncomfortably life-changing for me. Maybe He knows I can't handle that right now—maybe not ever. It could be that He is building perseverance and patience in me so that I might better recognize the beauty that comes from a "fervent, righteous prayer." Could it be that God wants to bless me even more than I can imagine at precisely the perfect time in my life?

Recently, I had a conversation with a special friend about prayer. I asked, "*How long is too long to pray for something?*" His first reply was, "*I don't know.*" I insisted that he give me an answer even if it might be wrong. After a brief wave of silence, his answer came as if from the heart of God. "*No amount of time is too long . . . even if it takes a lifetime to be answered.*" Luke 11:10 stirs me to pray with persistence and confidence.

> "For everyone who asks receives; and he who seeks
> finds; and to him who knocks it will be opened."
> Luke 11:10 (NASB)

My friend's reply may seem overwhelming and disheartening to some people. However, the words reminded me of the hope I have in my God. The hope that He always listens, always protects, and always answers. Even if the answer takes a lifetime . . . keep praying.

A Skinny Kid from Brooklyn

I've always been captivated with super heroes—Wonder Woman, Spiderman, The Incredible Hulk, and Batman. So, it was really no surprise when I got overly excited about seeing the new film, *Captain America: The First Avenger*. I admit that I didn't know much about the mysterious captain, but I did some homework and was fascinated by the story line. Seeing the movie was the highlight of my weekend. I loved it because I saw such a stunning parallel between the life of Steven Rogers a.k.a. as Captain America and the life of Christians . . . before and after their transformation.

Steven Rogers desperately wanted to serve in the United States Army during World War II. Time after time, he was turned away as unfit and unwanted because of various physical ailments and shortcomings. He had an understanding within that he was alive for a greater purpose. When presented with the opportunity to become something greater, Steven Rogers asked "*Why me?* The reply, "*Because a weak man knows the value of strength; knows the value of power.*" Before receiving Christ, we are not unlike Steven Rogers—weak, defenseless, unworthy. Deep inside our hearts, we surely realize that without Him, we are defeated; headed for a life of difficulty and tragedy veiled in the promise of death rather than eternal life.

Because someone believed in Steven Rogers, his dreams of helping in the war effort came true. He willingly underwent the transformation process in order to become all that he could be for the cause. He gained strength and a vision to fight against evil with good. Along with his new physique and mindset, he was labeled Captain America. The captain immediately set out to "save the world" one mission at a time. When he met up with Red Skull for the first time, his enemy asked, "*What makes you so special?*" Captain America answered, "*Nothing. I'm just a skinny kid from Brooklyn.*" He recognized that his power wasn't dependent on how special he was, but what he believed about himself. When we are saved, our focus and life undergo a radical change as shown in 2 Corinthians 5:17:

> "Therefore if anyone is in Christ, he is a new creation;
> the old things passed away; behold, new things have
> come." (NASB)

When we are called—set apart, God gives us special gifts and abilities to become the super warriors that He needs on the battlefield. The gifts vary and may be used in a million different ways, but they are all vital to the heartbeat of the Great Commission. As we travel through life, hopefully we will embrace Matthew 5:17,

> "Let your light shine before men in such as way that
> they may see your good works, and glorify your Father
> who is in heaven." (NASB)

I have never been anything special and people may wonder what my real purpose even is. I find myself asking why God and close friends believe in my goodness and abilities. Somebody bigger than you and I reached straight down from heaven and touched me. He placed His Spirit of power and fire within me and I've never been the same. God loved me enough—*a chubby girl from Payneville* to choose me . . . to transform me . . . to use me.

Any Way YOU Want Me

"But now, o LORD, You are our Father.
We are the clay, and You our Potter; and all of us are
the work of Your hand." Isaiah 64:8 (NASB)

From a very young age, children are conditioned to think about what they want to be when they grow up. Ballerinas, professional athletes, doctors, lawyers, teachers, artists, preachers . . . the list goes on and on. Down deep inside, we have a desire to build toward that dream of being someone and doing something with our life. Capturing the dreams and making them a reality is the defining moments in our lives.

Once upon a time, I had two plans for my future. The first plan was to become an astronaut. I was intrigued with the sun, moon, and stars. The thought of zooming through space had a certain glamorous appeal to me. I wanted to meet Neil Armstrong, Buzz Aldrin, and John Glenn. After all, they had all been where no man had been before. My second plan was to be a farmer's wife. That life would be simple yet complex. I envisioned baking bread, cookies, pies, and cakes. I wanted to start my mornings off with a tall glass of creamy milk—straight from the jersey cow. My farmer would kiss me on the cheek and promise to return to me at lunch. In my mind's eye, I pictured my charming farmhouse surrounded by prize winning rosebushes and tulips; framed with a white picket fence.

While I was busy making my plans, someone bigger than me was making plans as well. Someone who "looks to the ends of the earth and sees everything under the heavens." Job 28:24 (NASB) Someone who "knows my words before they are on my tongue." Psalm 139:4 (NASB) Someone who "is greater than my heart and knows all things." I John 3:20 (NASB)

In 1956, Elvis Presley recorded a song called *Any Way You Want Me*. Honestly, this was an Elvis Presley song that had slipped by me. Hearing it was like discovering a treasure that had been available my entire life. As I listened to the words, one verse in particular stood out. "In your hand my heart is clay, to take and mold as you may. I'm what you make me, you've only to take me, and in your arms I will stay." The message in this song parallels with what should be my attitude of submission toward the Father's hand in my life.

Needless to say, I didn't become an astronaut. It seems the Father had different ideas for my destiny. I'm a teacher in a small public school. I only see rockets on television and I've never met an astronaut. I know several farmers, but I'm not married to them. I'm a single lady with no rosebushes, tulips, or promises of lunchtime reunions. Does this mean I didn't capture my dream or meet my full potential? I don't think so. I believe it means that the Potter took me in His mighty hands, molded me, and carried me far beyond any expectation I could place on myself. Because of His presence in my life, I have no fear for the future. "For I know the plans I have for you," declares the LORD, "plans for welfare and not for calamity to give you a future and a hope." Jeremiah 29:11 (NASB)

Lights, Camera, Action!

"Therefore, we are ambassadors of Christ, as though
God were making an appeal through us; we beg you
on behalf of Christ, be reconciled to God."
2 Corinthians 5:20 (NASB)

One of my favorite things to do is watch old movies. Among
my favorites are *Little Women, Gone with the Wind, Meet Me in
St. Louis,* and *Roman Holiday.* The leading lady and leading man
always capture my attention and I'm quickly carried away by their
story. In my eyes, they represent the heartbeat of the movie and
determine whether I actually continue watching it or not. In a
sense, they either make or break the film for me.

Gregory Peck and Audrey Hepburn were dynamite in *Roman
Holiday.* They epitomized everything that a leading lady and
leading man should. Charisma, charm, mystery, humor, love, and
chemistry. No one else could have pulled off those roles the way
Peck and Hepburn did. They were the perfect compliment for

one another and sent the film into extreme success. They were the *ambassadors* for the movie and they served the part well. I've always dreamed of being a leading lady. Not so much in a movie, but in real life. The flawless beauty that turns heads, ends up happy in the end, and always "gets her guy." I would be a real ambassador for love and happiness. The guy would be tall, dark, and romantic—Gregory Peck.

Realistically, I know that someone isn't going to sweep me off my feet and whisk me around Rome on a motorized scooter. I understand that I'm not going to be the dream girl that wins Academy Awards. I'm never going to be a princess ignoring my royal duties for a few days. It isn't likely that a newspaper reporter is going to secretly write about my every move. It seems even less likely that I'm going to fall in love Hollywood style. However, I do have a far more important role to play. You see, I am one of God's leading ladies. He has prepped me for opening night by giving me words to speak, blessing me with gifts of service, and strengthening me to endure the race of life. All of my goodness comes from God.

> "Whoever speaks, is to do so as one who is speaking
> the utterances of God; whoever serves, is to do so
> as one who is serving by the strength which God
> supplies; so that in all things God may be glorified
> through Jesus Christ, to whom belongs the glory and
> dominion forever and ever." I Peter 4:11 (NASB)

End of Story

I love to talk about life. Life is a series of mountaintop and valley experiences, and I ache to talk about them all. With that loves comes a bad habit. Sometimes, I just don't know when to stop. I know that I wear some people out with my nonstop analyzing, worrying, and thinking. Most people just simply listen. A few add fuel to the fire and keep me going. But, there is one that will tell me, "Stop it. Stop it now." Don't get me wrong, he listens intently. However, when I round the corner and head back to the same story with the same details, he refuses to walk the road with me again.

On more than one occasion, his reaction has hurt my feelings. You could even say that it puts me into a sour mood, and he further adds salt to the wound by calling me a "sour puss." So, not only has he basically told me to shut up, but he has called me a name. My logical conclusion is that he doesn't care enough to listen to me. He obviously doesn't love me.

Recently, I was talking to him about my day. I described it as nothing short of devastating. I shared with my friend once, and he sat and looked me in the eye for nearly two hours. He offered encouragement, understanding, and patience. I finished, he hugged me, and the subject was changed. I wasn't satisfied. I decided to tell him all over again. Maybe he didn't care enough the first time. He may not have clearly heard me. Maybe, just maybe I had left out some important element of the story that he needed to know. Being the good friend that he is, he persevered a little longer than usual, but I could tell I was pushing my luck. Finally, he said, "You are finished. Stop." I hung on passionately and tried to speed talk my way through. Although I tried to ignore him, my efforts were in vain. I had tested his patience and he would have no more of it. "No. No more, Karen. End of story." He had rendered me powerless and my eyes bulged with tears.

When I lay down in my bed that night, I realized how excessively stressed out I had become in the process of "telling" him my story. I had nearly worked myself into a panic attack. I had a raging headache and my chest felt tight. As I lay there in my emotional fog, I realized that I was somewhat relieved that he had told me to stop. Somehow, he knew that I couldn't be allowed to go on. He had saved me from myself. I was literally worn out. I had whined and worried to the point of no return. I had begged him to give me more than anyone was really capable of giving. The problem I had faced was bigger than me or any remedy he might dream up.

I have to learn to close my mouth and recognize the counsel that is being given. Whether it is words of wisdom, a kind touch, or a loving gesture, being still has its time and place. Though his method seemed cold at first, my friend knew that he had to shock me in order for me to listen. I could not continue to be a big crybaby . . . it was getting me nowhere. I understand now that it was his love and concern for me that motivated him to "shut me up."

I can only imagine how God feels when I sit down here spouting off my requests to Him. I drown out any hope of hearing His answers because I just keep flooding Him with details and yearnings. Flooding Him with things He already knows. My goodness, shouldn't it be enough to know that He loves and cares for me more than anything? I can almost hear God saying, "Karen, stop. No more . . . end of story." His true heart to reach me is found in the words of Psalm 46:10a (NASB): "Cease striving and know that I am God . . ." What a calming reassurance to know He is my God.

He doesn't want me to be still because He is sick of hearing from me. Sometimes, He wants to hear me through my thoughts . . . my tears . . . my heart. God desperately wants to work in my life and bring me to a deeper understanding of His presence in my life. He desires to lift me up through the silence and teach me to depend on Him and His unwavering goodness. Once I give it all up to God and close my mouth, I truly can rest in the fact that He is the Author . . . the One who will ultimately write the end of the story.

Four Pounds of Ooey Gooey Goodness

"But just as you abound in everything, in faith and
utterance and knowledge and in all earnestness and in
the love we inspired in you, see that you abound in this
gracious work also." 2 Corinthians 8:11-14 (NASB)

I bake chocolate chip cookies for many different people. I do this because I enjoy baking and it shows my love for others. There are a few people in my life that have been the recipients of chocolate chip cookies and there is an understanding between us. I've told them when their container is empty; they can return it to be filled back up. One friend has managed to latch onto two containers so my baking for him is nearly endless. I admit that I wouldn't have it any other way.

So, the container idea has taken off and recently, I gifted another special person with a chocolate chip cookie box. My good friend and co-worker, Kelly Wathen was diagnosed with leukemia during the 2010 Christmas holiday. Kelly has struggled for months as he has endured treatments and side effects of the medicine and the leukemia. For several months, Kelly didn't desire much in the line of food and that was certainly understandable. However, I went out on a limb and baked him a batch of chocolate chip cookies. I had my crafty nieces design a box with hunting stickers to store the cookies in. Honestly, I thought it was a long shot that he would even want to eat the cookies. I gave them to him and explained the process for receiving more cookies.

Three days later, Kelly hunted me down at a mutual friend's house to return the cookie box. It warmed my heart to know that he wanted more cookies. I baked him another batch and he convinced the principal of our school to bring him to my house to pick them up. Again, within a few days, the box was returned. I went to Kroger and bought fresh chocolate chips, brown sugar, and vanilla. I filled the box—to the brim with cookies. It has become my mission to keep Kelly with a fresh supply of chocolate chip cookies for as long as he desires to have them.

I just always seem to have what I need to bless the lives of others with my baking. As I bake more and more, my supplies are increasing and on any given day, I can whip up a batch of my secret recipe chocolate chip cookies. One day, I was teaching Math and my principal walked into my classroom. She had Kelly's cookie box. Needless to say, it was empty *again.* I was so excited! Another opportunity to sweeten his life. Not only did she have his cookie box, but she also had chocolate chips—a 72 ounce bag of chocolate chips! The message that Kelly sent was: "*Tell her that this doesn't mean she has to bake more cookies for me.*" Even in the midst of his great trial, Kelly gave back to me in a way that he knew would touch my life and the lives of others. He is always the one putting a smile back on my face . . . reminding me that he is still on top of his game.

My original gift of chocolate chip cookies was complimented by his gift of chocolate chips. That gift will impact the lives of many people that I love because I will be able to bake dozens of cookies from that bag of chocolate chips. The love and the sweetness have multiplied and the giving has far surpassed anything that I originally had in my plans or my heart. A ridiculously jumbo bag of chocolate chips will help create the ooey gooey goodness that puts a sweet feeling in the tummy of many people.

Does Your Heart Understand What Your Head Knows?

When God created us, He gave us an intricate organ to use for thinking and reasoning. It is through the brain that we can read books, solve intricate problems, and make life-changing decisions. Our brain helps us learn right from wrong and it allows us to complete every movement our body makes. We can build great knowledge and store it away in the depths of our brain and use it for a multitude of things. It probably isn't necessary to convince anyone that the brain is a beautiful thing.

I started reading about Jesus long before I entered into a real relationship with Him. The stories were interesting and even entertaining, but they were just that—stories. After I was saved at the age of seven, I found that I was hungering for God's Word in a different way. I had a longing to better understand the Truth and apply it to my life. I was curious. If I studied the Bible, could I have what the Psalmist spoke of in Psalm 119:30 (NASB)? "I have chosen the faithful way, I have placed your ordinances before me."

I was able to retell the story of Noah's Ark, Moses and the Ten Commandments, Joshua and the Battle of Jericho, The Good Samaritan, and Jesus Feeding the Five Thousand. I had incredible Sunday school teachers. They encouraged me to memorize key Scriptures. However, I realized that I only memorized the Scriptures to receive a reward—a mustard seed locket, a silver dollar, or a Tootsie Roll pop. These rewards had temporal value, and were lost or used up in a matter of time. I had the knowledge, but lacked complete understanding and devotion. Simply going through the motions of reading God's Word was honestly not enough to light my path or transform my perspective. I wasn't doing a bad thing. I was just storing the information in the wrong spot. Slowly but surely, I realized that I was embracing a religious experience rather than a deep, committed relationship.

I wanted my heart to understand what my head knew. My intellectual connection to Jesus Christ motivated me to fill the God sized shape in my heart and create an emotional connection to Him. He literally opened my eyes and filled my heart with His promises and love. I found an infinitely precious place deep within to lock away the treasures of His Word. The true joy of my salvation emerged when I took hold of the Scripture, held on for dear life, and remembered, "Your Word I have treasured in my heart, that I may not sin against You." Psalm 119:11 (NASB)

"Hey, That's My Laugh! You Can't Do That!"

Just about everyone has lasting memories of their favorite cartoon. For some reason, we attach significance to a cartoon character and cling to the things connected to that character. There is something sweetly sentimental about recalling famous lines and antics that take place during cartoon episodes. When it seems the world is falling in around us, those crazy characters put a certain pizazz back in our day and we smile . . . or quite possibly, we laugh out loud!

The things we love most about cartoon characters are their endearing character traits and outward appearance. Consider Tweety Bird: the sweet, precious yellow bird fluttered around and called out, "*I 'tawt I taw a puddy tat!*" And there's Wile E. Coyote and the Roadrunner—one was full of perservance and the other was brimming over with clever wit. Who could forget Chilly Willy's distinctive voice and deadpan personality? Even Puss in

Boots finds his way into many hearts with his cunning charm, impressive sword skills, and enchanting stare. If your emotions have yet to be stirred, visit the deepest caverns of your mind and you might just hear the hysterical laughter of none other than Woody the Woodpecker! That laugh was, if nothing else, contagious.

As a youngster, I was a giggler rather than a laugher. I didn't have it in me to really burst out in a good 'ole belly laugh. I did get into my share of trouble in grade school for falling into fits of giggling. There was no rhyme or reason for the giggling and the source could have been any number of things. I also found myself being reprimanded for lying in bed with my best friend giggling. Now, these episodes were different because I had a friend giggling with me—that made everthing all the more humorous. My dad would come to the door and say, "*Girls, pipe it down and go to sleep.*" Needless to say, this only caused more giggling. This type of giggling eventually led to tears of happiness, and that felt awfully good.

I heard recently that a person should laugh out loud no less than twelve times each day in order to gain positive health benefits. Wow . . . twelve times? Really? At one time, this would have seemed like an impossibility for me. I just simply didn't laugh out loud. However, I'm beginning to see that laughing does in fact have some benefits for my general outlook on life. A few weeks ago, I was having dinner with a friend. One of his greatest talents is voice impersonations. In fact, he has created about eight inner personalities to entertain with. As I was chowing down on my burger listening to him carry on a three way conversation, something he said struck me like nothing else he had ever said. He laughed and then I literally laughed out loud in a restaurant . . . a restaurant with other people sitting in close proximity.

I shocked myself and my friend. It was extremely out of character for me. I will a little embarassed, but that feeling quickly passed as I recognized a new found feeling in my heart—I had reached a new plane. Looking back, I do not even know what I laughed at, but I did come to a few conclusions. It made me feel extremely good on the inside, it changed the whole climate of the evening, and it connected me in a unique way with the person I was laughing with. Proverbs 17:22a (NASB) says,

"A joyful heart is good medicine . . ."

Laughter truly does do a body good. For the moments directly following the laughter, one is overcome with joy and excitement . . . peace and contentment. You find yourself anxious for the next great thing to happen just so you can laugh out loud again. Just try it and you will see that I am telling the truth.

Those classic Woody the Woodpecker cartoons kept us in stitches for sure and we are forever connected to the zany bird and his incessant laughter. Woody the Woodpecker said, *"Hey, that's my laugh! You can't take it!"* He didn't want to be duplicated—only imitated! God has a completely different idea about laughter. He created laughter and He fully intends for us to laugh loud and often. God loves the sound of our laughter and He expects us to give it away to others. I believe that our laughter is a direct reflection of God's happiness and delight. So, what are you waiting for? Laugh out loud . . . . because you can.

If It's Out of Sight, Don't Worry About It

My grandparents owned an appliance and furniture store for many years. When they made the decision to retire, my parents bought the store and determined themselves to continue the family legacy. At the time of the purchase, I was in the midst of figuring out what it was I wanted to do with the rest of my life. I had just completed a year of college and had decided that it wasn't the life for me. So, I was drawn into the family business. My responsibilities varied and I was barely qualified to complete any of them. As a matter of fact, I literally had to learn *everything*. From the get go, I had three strikes against me. I was terrible in math, which was not good considering I was expected to complete all of the bookwork and record keeping tasks. I wasn't a people person—a little scary considering a job in the public meant, well . . . dealing with people. I had no idea how to diagnose appliance problems or locate a part for a customer, which just happened to be what about half of the people who walked through the doors wanted. This was definitely going to be a rocky ride.

Although he had retired, my grandfather came to the store every single day. Around 10:00 A.M., he would show up, fill his coffee cup, sit down behind the counter, and wait. He would anxiously wait for a customer to come through the doors. I dreaded seeing him come because quite frankly, he scared me. He never smiled, he grunted instead of speaking, he was often short-tempered if you asked a question, and he had this way of looking at me as if he could see to the very deepest fiber of my soul. He knew that I was a complete novice when it came to the appliance business and having him sit behind me in the midst of customer relations was worse than anything I could imagine. I loved him, but I didn't *know* him.

As I faced customer after customer that first steamy summer, I felt more inadequate to fulfill my responsibilities. People were asking for agitator dogs and oven thermostats and dryer timers and icemaker gears. My frustration was hitting a dangerous level. My grandfather followed me to the parts department one day. I was frantic—trying to locate the correct bake element for an oven. I felt him breathing down my neck and I wanted to cry. Finally, he spoke. *"Well, do you know which one you need?"* My shattered reply, *"Not really."* He reached up and pulled the bake element down and handed it to me. It was at this moment in time that my grandfather and I formed a bond.

He continued to follow me to the parts department every single time a customer needed a part. He taught me where everything was based on my height and arm length. When I couldn't locate something, he would say, *"If it's out of sight, don't worry about it."* Every part I ever needed was within my range. I still have no idea what was on the very top shelves of the parts department. I honestly never needed anything from those shelves, and I finally grew less and less curious about what was housed there. I was comfortable in my "range."

As I move through my daily routine, I think about how comfortable I have become with the things I can see without making much of an effort . . . the things that don't cause me too much of a strain. I look out for my own problems, interests, and dreams. I become caught up in the ministries that come easy for me and I feel secure dealing with the people I have always dealt with. Honestly, I don't feel too awfully curious about what is just beyond my fingertips—those things that *concern others*. Philippians 2:4 (NASB) commands:

"Do not merely look out for your own personal
interests, but also for the interests of others."

I'm prone to wonder, *"How many distressing things are just out of my sight that I just choose not to worry about?"* Jesus consistently placed himself in the middle of gravely ill people. He fellowshipped with sinners. Jesus did not ignore what was just beyond His sight for anything—He did worry about it and He was certainly interested. Jesus was in the business of looking above and beyond any and all situations to lift up that person who needed Him the most. So, maybe I'm not that tall, but I can stand on my tip-toes and bless someone else. I can use those forgotten muscles to stretch beyond my arm span and make someone else's day.

My Mask: PARANOIA

When Halloween rolls around, it is sure to conjure up some type of memories in your head. One memory I have is choosing my costume each year. My number one rule was: *no mask!* I couldn't stand the smothering feeling that a mask gave me when I put it on. One year, I broke my number one rule and wore a Wonder Woman mask. Sure, I looked like a first class super hero, but I was miserable . . . absolutely miserable all night long. The heavy plastic mask made my face sweat and I'm pretty sure I was deprived of necessary oxygen flow that night. Plus, I spent more time lifting the mask up so my loved ones would know which precious trick-or-treater I was than actually staying disguised.

Through the years, masks have brought on a different meaning for me. It's those imaginary masks that we all wear at times that can truly leave a person suffocating. Oh, we wear them for a variety of reasons—*self-esteem, social acceptance, mystery, hiding, faking* . . . need I go on? Whatever the reason, the mask cripples us and robs us of our joy. Along the way, we may even hurt other people. In my case,

I mostly hurt myself with the mask that I wear. It is called the *mask of paranoia.*

When I'm dressed as paranoia, it is nowhere near as pretty Wonder Woman. In fact, it is downright unappealing to anyone around me. As I have examined the common causes for my paranoia, I have been enlightened. Carefully, I have narrowed down the top six paranoia influences in my life: *stress, worry, fear, negative self-worth, overactive imagination,* and *doubt.*

Simply put, I sabotage many opportunities for happiness and fulfilling experiences. Rather than accepting things as they really are, I go to work trying to analyze things that are not even a part of the picture—things that may or may not ever enter the quotient. I decide that people are acting different or avoiding me. I assume that things are going on that I am not being given information about. Of course, I conclude that things are being hidden from me. Suddenly, I am walking on egg shells and trying to decipher every move and word by the individuals involved. My overactive imagination reigns supreme and I begin to question my value to others. I try to be everything to them and I fail in a monumental way. It is in trying to be everything to them that I lose myself. I get so trapped in a cycle of being what I think they expect that I'm no longer the person they loved to begin with. Thanks to the unattractive mask I hide behind, they sit across from me at dinner and silently wonder, "*Who are you and what did you do with the girl I love?*" I confronted a friend recently and asked, "*What do you expect from me?*" In my paranoia, I believed I wasn't being enough or doing enough. He replied, "*Just be you.*" How simple . . . no mask required!

As I face each new day and accept the challenges coming toward me, I am slowly realizing that a life free of paranoia could be quite enjoyable. I haven't completely destroyed the mask of paranoia, but I have the desire to, and that is a huge step. The people that are closest to me are quite blunt when I need to come back to reality and give up the disguise. So, in their way, they are helping me to heal. Does their method sometimes seem harsh? Yes. However, I can admit that God is using them as an instrument to reach me in my state of need. I know that the healing I truly need comes through God. When I stress or worry, I can go to Him with my needs and live in the confidence of the cross. When I feel worthless and overcome with doubt, He fills me with His richness, glory, and grace. He can swoop in and save my day, if I only make my needs known.

> "Be anxious for nothing, but in everything by prayer
> and supplication with thanksgiving let your requests be
> made known to God." Philippians 4:6 (NASB)

My Pants Are Too Short!

"Let your gentle spirit be known to all men. The Lord
is near." Philippians 4:5 (NASB)

My grandfather was slow to anger and had the patience of
Job. I never heard him raise his voice, he never lashed out in anger
at someone else, and he never lost his temper with us kids. Sam
Epperson was a perfect example of *even temperament* and *patience*.
Since my grandfather drew from an unending well of serenity, he
handled difficult situations and irritating people with gentleness
and kindness. If only I had inherited those qualities from my
grandfather . . . if only.

Dr. Bruce Banner was the brilliant scientist that transformed
into the Incredible Hulk under extreme emotional stress. Banner
was controlled—responsible—even highly intelligent in most
instances. However, when something went wrong, you better
watch out! One moment a wide-eyed man of wisdom and the
next an emotional basket case.

Before anyone could figure out what was really going on, Dr. Bruce Banner turned green, burst out of his shirt, and suddenly had a terrible case of high waters. He absolutely blew up into a fit of rage and it was 80's television at its dramatic best. Was it a lack of self-control or a passion to turn a wrong into a right? What did he accomplish by unleashing his emotional stress to the point of transfiguration? How might the results have been different if he had allowed Proverbs 15:1 to direct his thoughts and actions?

> "A gentle answer turns away wrath, but a harsh word
> stirs up anger." Proverbs 15:1 (NASB)

Better yet, how might the results of the upheavals in my life be different and more positive if I were to focus my attention on Proverbs 15:1? Rather than resembling my grandfather when a particularly difficult situation arises, I am more prone to embody the angst and wrath of the Incredible Hulk. Unfortunately, when I boil over with emotional anxiety, people do not view it as they did when the gargantuan green monster fell apart at the seams. Rather, they may have a spirit of cautiousness or an uneasy feeling about how I might react. They might avoid me or prefer not to invite me into the more intimate details of their life. They might even walk on eggshells to prevent me from becoming emotional.

I have no desire to walk through life being compared to the Incredible Hulk. I'm not an infamous scientist that can blame a bad science experiment on my shortcomings. Green is not one of my favorite colors and I prefer that my pants not randomly creep up my shins. Being forever watchful and mindful of the things that trigger my emotions seems a great place to start in taming the green giant that lurks inside me. Staying strong in courage rather than being a slave to my emotions will keep me true to His call on my life. Dr. Bruce Banner once said, *"I want to make sure that never happens again. I want to be Dr. Banner, not Dr. Jekyll."* This is a true sentiment for someone like me to cling to as I strive not to be guided by outside stress or inward heartache. Rather, may I be compelled to allow the Holy Spirit and the goodness of God to dwell in me and flow from me as a fount of strength and love.

Friends for Life

"A friend loves at all times . . ."
Proverbs 17:17a (NASB)

I was 11 years old when I met Chad. We had an instant connection and I will always believe that he was the brother God sent to me. We saw the best in each other. He was cute, sweet, humorous, and talented. He was happiness, fun, kindness, and love. Chad was my kindred spirit.

My fondest memories of Chad are connected to Raymond Baptist Church. His father was my pastor and his mother was my youth leader. It might have seemed more natural that I would be best friends with the sister he brought along with him, but that wasn't meant to be. He would slip into church with his baseball cap pulled down over his eyes. He would slide into the pew and sit still as a statue. I knew to watch or I would miss it. He would finally peek out from under that cap and wink at me. If I was really lucky, he would stick his tongue out at me, too! Sometimes he played his trumpet while my sister played the piano and I loved it! He would always pick me to be on his team even though I couldn't hit a ball that far and my running was mediocre.

Chad was a loyal friend and I told him that many times in letters and poems. He would say that my words made a young boy like him cry. It was easy to be honest with Chad and even easier to say beautiful things about him. In return for the letters and poems, he drew me pictures and he made me giggle. He had no mercy; even when I couldn't breathe, he kept goofing and I kept laughing. Chad was brave and he was never afraid to say that he loved me. He is most likely the reason that some of the greatest friendships in my life have been with males.

I stood beneath a tree with Chad one Sunday afternoon and we pledged to be friends for life. Friends for life . . .

A few short years after that pledge, I went to college and Chad's family left Raymond Baptist Church. Ironically, we both wound up in Bowling Green, but I only saw him twice while there. Chad never left my heart and his passion for life continued to inspire me as year after year passed. I would recall something he said or an expression he made. Sometimes the recollection would make me laugh and sometimes it would make me cry.

Eventually, I lost count of how many years passed since seeing him. I reminisced about him. I pondered a reunion with him. I planned to write him a letter. I figured I would give him a call. I just knew that I would see Chad again someday. I heard things about him through the years . . . he was working, he was married, he was happy, he was sad, he cared about me, he missed me, he was all grown up and so was I.

Chad slipped through my fingers. He disappeared just like that. Six years ago, my family was celebrating Mother's Day and I received a phone call. Chad was dead. He was gone, and my plans were gone with him. Neither of us could have known that life was so limited for him.

"Yet you do not know what your life will be like
tomorrow. You are just a vapor that appears for a little
while and then vanishes away." James 4:14 (NASB)

I never got to tell Chad that even in my grown-up heart; he filled a place that no one else could. He had given me a special kind of happiness that I would never experience again in this lifetime. He was and forever will be ... *my friend for life.*

The King We Never Knew

"Therefore, I the prisoner of the Lord, implore you to
walk in a manner worthy of the calling with which
you have been called." Ephesians 4:1 (NASB)

Back in 1982, Graceland opened for public tours. It took me
29 years to finally make my pilgrimage to the hallowed grounds of
rock and roll. My friend Stephen made the trip with me and it was
an adventure! We were so excited about standing in Elvis' home
and seeing memorabilia that once belonged to him. It was a moving
experience to visit and imagine a day in the life of Elvis Presley.
As we strolled from the kitchen to the jungle room, I pictured
Elvis chowing down on a peanut butter and banana sandwich. My
mind's eye allowed me to envision him playing with Lisa Marie
in the floor. It felt as if I were a best friend of the king enjoying a
casual visit at his mansion.

One part of the tour was located in the Meditation Garden
where Elvis and some of his closest family members are buried. We

stood there and pondered the life that the King of Rock and Roll had led. Before I arrived that day, the words I would have used to describe him were . . . . *handsome, talented, musical, charming, wealthy,* and *entertaining.* In reality, these are all appropriate characteristics to attach to Elvis Presley. After all, the Elvis I saw was the suave singer. He was the entertainer that women swooned over and men wanted to imitate. Elvis Presley was a fashion icon and social butterfly. Elvis need only show up and excitement escalated to new levels. Stephen is more of an Elvis expert than I am, but I always figured I knew enough to get by. Actually, I believed I knew mostly everything worth knowing. As we walked away from Graceland, Stephen and I had both drawn the same conclusion: We didn't really know the king at all.

Elvis was a true humanitarian—often giving away the very vehicle he was riding in at any given time. He gave countless gifts of cash, jewelry, automobiles and homes to those who were close to him. On one single day, Elvis Presley donated $40,000 to various charity organizations. This was certainly a man with more than singing on his mind. Yet, I'm almost positive that no one truly embraced this Elvis. Although he unselfishly gave to those in need, people were more concerned with the glitz and glamour of a rockin' movie star. It's sad and even difficult to believe that it took his death for people to honor and recognize him for things beyond his dancing and singing. Things that left as much or more of an impression as listening to hits like *Love Me Tender, Hound Dog,* and *Jailhouse Rock.* If we were to admit it, we know more of the words to his songs than anything he supported or stood for.

My experience at Graceland found me thinking about the legacy I will leave behind someday. I suppose there are the things that family and friends will never forget about me—*chocolate chip cookies, loyal allegiance, honesty, sense of humor.* However, do I strive each and every day to build a legacy that speaks of my love for God . . . His Son . . . His vision? I must examine my heart and determine whether I want to be known for the "me" things or the God things. And as I do that, I may find myself living out Colossians 1:10 (NASB) more and more:

"So that you will walk in a manner worthy of the
Lord, to please Him in all respects, bearing fruit in
every good work and increasing in the
knowledge of God."

Elvis did not hold the key to an unattainable mystery. He is not the only person to understand the revelation that we are here for a purpose greater than ourselves. While he may not have been perfect, Elvis Presley was charitable at a deeper degree than he may have ever been given credit. Today I seek to be driven by the motivation of honoring God in honest, sincere ways. I hope to realize that the last $10 I have may indeed serve someone else better than it serves me. I desire for my selfish ambitions to be blotted out and all my adoration be fixed upon loving my Lord in a tender way through pleasing acts of kindness.

"Try to learn what is pleasing to the Lord."
Ephesians 5:10 (NASB)

When Our Thoughts Become Words

"He who guards his mouth and tongue, guards his soul
from troubles." Proverbs 21:23 (NASB)

I was never the outdoorsy type, but there were things about
the outdoors that I cherished as a child . . . trees, mud puddles,
clouds, acorns, butterflies, lightning bugs, and dandelions. I loved
the dandelions when they were puffy and white! I would feverishly
pluck as many out of the ground as I could and make a bouquet
that resembled a huge snowball. With all my might, I would make a
wish and blow the seeds. The seeds would scatter and travel on the
wings of the wind. Indeed, it was a breathtaking sight!

I had a cousin that always broke the rules. She did what everyone
else was doing, but she had to do it just a little bit differently. One
day she picked a dandelion, got right up in my face, and blew
hard enough that the stem was rendered naked in an instant. Just
like that, the seeds were tickling my nose, coating my tongue, and
scratching my eyes. I was so mad that I pushed her down on the
ground. She laughed and I cried.

As I recall this moment with my cousin, I think about how the seeds could be compared to words. I love to talk to people. As much as I try to use my words to love, encourage, and build up, I realize I make grave mistakes at times. No doubt, I have made someone cry over my words. I'm sure that I have made someone feel inadequate because of my words. I am often sassy or sharp with my answers. Sometimes, people might even be able to tell that I'd rather not be talking to them at all because of the emptiness of my words. I have the power to keep my thoughts to myself or verbalize them. When I verbalize them, they become as the seed of a dandelion—spreading out to be a positive force or invading the calm that someone else was perfectly content with.

Every day is an opportunity for me to put a smile on someone's face. Every hour is a chance for me to heal a broken heart. Every minute is the right time to touch the life of someone else . . . with my words. Words matter to other people in a hugely critical way. May my words be few and may the words that I do speak be as gold to the one receiving them.

> "Like apples of gold in settings of silver is a word
> spoken in right circumstances." Proverbs 25:11

On The 8th Day He Created Cupcakes

I love nothing more than to bring happiness to people's lives through delectable creations—*cakes, cupcakes,* and *pies.* Friends and family have come to know that a visit from me usually carries the promise of their favorite dessert. These sugary gifts are my way of showing how much I love and care for them. Sometimes, I like to spoil myself a little bit and indulge in the baking that someone else does. Without too much regret, I once visited a cupcake shop three times in one week. I told one of my friends that I had eaten yet another cupcake and he replied, "*So?*" I feel especially happy when someone gives me the green light on eating sweets! However, I do wonder silently, *"Would he fall under the captivity of cupcakes with me if he were here?"* I know that the answer is, "Yes." He is the one friend that allows me to enjoy eating sweets without making me feel guilty. It is one of the things I love most about him. He knows I adore sweets; therefore, he doesn't send me on a guilt trip over it.

In my sugary comatose state, I convinced myself that I was frequenting the cupcake shop simply for the cupcakes. I was in fact, entering the gates of Heaven every time I went in and saw bowl upon bowl of fluffy icing. I made my way up to the pearly gates as the aroma of cupcakes took my breath away. It is difficult

to describe how overwhelmingly happy I was when I reached
the throne and took in all of the available cupcake flavors: *Death
By Chocolate, Lemon Blueberry, Salty Caramel, Caramel Apple, Red
Velvet, German Chocolate, Peanut Butter Banana Fluff,* and *Chocolate
Almond.* I was thinking, *"God sure does know how to spoil a girl!"*
Cupcakes—by far His greatest creation! Through my rendezvous
at the cupcake shop, He has taught me a lesson about my obsession
with sweets and my innate desire to spoil others.

The question is: *Why has God placed this love for sweets in my
heart?* I had a revelation when I was standing in the midst of
cupcake paradise yesterday. While my avenue of service to others
is baking sweets, the purpose goes beyond the burst of chocolate
and powdered sugar that people experience when they bite into
a dessert I have made. Long after the cookie container is empty
and houses only tiny crumbs—little memories left from famous
recipe chocolate chip cookies, something lingers in the heart of
the sweets recipient. The sweetness I showed from the depths of
my heart.

If truth be known, it is not the actual dessert that makes the people
feel special. Honestly, I believe it's the fact that I thought of them. I
considered what their favorite sweet is and then I took the time to
make it for them. I not only used ingredients from my cabinets, but
I used ingredients from my heart—*love, tenderness, honesty, creativity,*
and *unselfishness.* Beyond these things, I get the opportunity to
spend special time with the individual when I deliver their box of
goodies. I pray that my words are guarded—pure—good. I pray
that those I spend time with feel a sweetness that comes from my
soul to theirs. May both the tangible and intangible gifts that I bear
when I go visiting, be constant reminders of a sweet goodness in
the life of those I love the most. Lord use me to live out Proverbs
16:24 (NASB): "Pleasant words are a honeycomb, sweet to the soul
and healing to the bones."

"Dorothy, I Have a Feeling We're Not in Kentucky Anymore!"

Webster defines *vacation* as *a period spent away from home and work in rest and recreation.* I'm quite sure that if I were to dissect the word and read the fine print, it also includes "letting go, not worrying, and focusing on the positive things in life." Recently, I went on a short vacation. I had visions of forgetting what was in Kentucky and never turning back—until I had to. For the people who know me best, it would come as no surprise that for the first three days of my vacation, the only thing I did do was worry . . . and think . . . and analyze. These *things* I was allowing to rob me of quality vacation time were in essence things I have no control over anyway. I didn't recognize my foolishness until a friend said to me, *"Karen, you are on vacation . . . go enjoy it."* It was as if the voice of God had thundered down from heaven:

"Come to Me, all who are weary and heavy-laden, and
I will give you rest. Take My yoke upon you and learn
from Me, for I am gentle and humble in heart, and you
will find rest for your souls. For My yoke is easy and
My burden is light." Matthew 11:28-30 (NASB)

So, on the fourth day of vacation, I woke up with a new spirit. I really did want to rest and meditate on the beauty around me. I realized that I was surrounded by things that are the total opposite of Kentucky. Sand, dolphins, oceans, jellyfish, lighthouses, pelicans, shrimp boats, shells, and harbors. These were the things that I couldn't overlook . . . the things that I couldn't take back home with me . . . the things I would long for when time moved me back to my regular routine.

I didn't think too much about home that day. Rather, I thought that it was really rather nice to visit another of God's awesome creations for a week. I believe I was pretty lucky to have seen a family of dolphins make their way across the ocean. I loved the experience of walking on the beach barefoot and feeling the coarse, wet sand squish between my toes. I was entranced as I observed how the sunlight danced upon the foamy water. Nothing quite compares to saying, "*Goodnight*" to the world with all of that staring back at me.

I managed to do the right thing and *enjoy* my vacation. After all, God did have a plan when he put the ocean in place . . . from the beginning of time: "The earth was formless and void, and darkness was over the face of the deep, and the Spirit of God was moving over the surface of the waters." Genesis 1:2 (NASB)

It certainly was a respite from the ordinary, mundane life that I feel I lead most of the time. Vacation was a wake-up call for me and probably mirrored Dorothy's amazement when she woke up in Munchkinland. Most definitely, I had a strange feeling and declared *"I'm definitely not in Kentucky anymore."*

All Spatulas Are Not Created Equal

It was a typical day for me. I got a "b in my bonnet" to bake chocolate chip cookies. I had methodically placed my arsenal of baking supplies on the counter . . . *silver measuring spoons, 4-cup measuring cup, Kitchen Aid mixer, pink spatula.* I was savoring the scent of butter and sugar as I came to my favorite part of the cookie baking process—stirring in the chocolate chips! I picked up my favorite spatula, the sassy pink one. I began to fold in the chocolate chips just like I always do and suddenly—SNAP!! The spatula cracked in half. I froze. Had I handled it differently than the previous 100 times? Was my cookie dough too thick? Could I patch the spatula and continue to use it?

Completely convinced that baking was over for the day, I felt a warm tear stream down my face. Its saltiness seemed to rob me of the sweet sensations I typically feel when baking. I couldn't imagine baking the batch of cookies without my beloved spatula. I was angry with myself for breaking the handle and I knew I could never replace it . . . sad, sad day. I put the broken spatula in a drawer with some of my cookbooks. I considered it a somewhat peaceful resting place for the precious utensil.

I reluctantly finished the cookies and my feelings were shot. Blah! For once in my life, I didn't want to deliver the cookies to the people I had been so enthusiastic about baking them for. As if stirring them with a wooden spoon rather than a pink spatula made any difference whatsoever. The people on the receiving end would certainly be none the wiser.

After I recovered from the initial shock and grief of losing one of my favorite tools, I decided to see what was available in the world of spatulas. After all, I wasn't going to be able to resurrect the broken one. The sooner I moved on, the better off I was going to be. I shared with a close friend about my spatula shopping and he found it rather amusing that I had been "surfing the net" for spatulas. I didn't let his teasing get to me. I knew that a new spatula would bring delight back into my heart about baking. I found the perfect set of spatulas and they could even be personalized! I didn't want to be selfish and impulsive about ordering them. Rather, I concluded that I needed to reflect on the fact that my joy of baking had nothing to do with me, but everything to do with the Lord and how I could use that gift for others. In time, my heart was singing a different tune as I better understood that my delight should come straight from the Lord:

"Delight yourself in the Lord; and He will give you the
desires of your heart." Psalms 37:4 (NASB)

I finally threw the broken spatula in the trash. Ironically, I didn't shed a tear over it. I believed that in time, the Lord would indeed give me the desires of my heart. In His time . . . His good and perfect time. A few months after the spatula saga, my birthday came around. My friend took me to birthday breakfast and surprised me with a pretty pink package. He had never asked what I wanted; so I was extremely curious as I opened the gift. Greater than the gift was the thoughtfulness that stood behind it. I pulled out not only one, but THREE personalized spatulas—small, medium, and large. While he had been teasing about my obsession with spatulas, he had orchestrated a plan to bring a smile to my face. I know that God worked through my friend to bring me the desire of my heart. He placed me in a waiting period to develop a greater character. For the second time in just a matter of months, I shed tears over something as simple as spatulas. The first were tears of selfishness and loss. The second were from joy, delight, and a changed heart.

"Create in me a clean heart, O God, and renew a steadfast spirit within me." Psalm 51:10 (NASB)

Was Martha ALL Bad??

On any given holiday, I spend the entire day prior to and the morning of the holiday in the kitchen. The kitchen is my comfort zone and it's where I put my creative ideas to the test. I love being up to my ears in confectioner's sugar, unsalted butter, cream cheese, and extra large eggs! The hum of my mixer is comforting and peaceful. I try to make everyone's favorite desserts; so they will be happy. As you may have guessed, everyone likes something different: *lemon blossoms, chocolate cake, coconut crème pie, chocolate chip cookies, carrot cake,* and *peanut butter pie.* This is my passion—feeding the hearts of loved ones through their tummies. It makes me glad for them to request their favorite.

I am often caught unaware with guests arriving—typically, I bite off more than I can chew. It is not unusual to find me with flour on my chin, cookie dough in my hair, and icing on my fingers—fifteen minutes from serving time. These guests are always of utmost importance to me, and it is my desire to serve them. I never want someone else to frost my cake or baby my cookies to the stage of perfection. Honestly, I do not want help; although any of my sisters, nieces, or nephews would gladly assist me. I am prone to recall Jesus' visit with Mary and Martha when I'm twirling around in the kitchen:

> " . . . a woman named Martha welcomed Him into her
> home. She had a sister called Mary, who was seated at
> the Lord's feet, listening to His word. But Martha was
> distracted with all her preparations; and she came up
> to Him and said, 'Lord, do you not care that my sister
> has left me to do all the serving alone? Then tell her to
> help me.'" Luke 10:38b-40 (NASB)

When I read that Scripture, I pause and ask, *"Was there any point where Martha was enjoying her service?" "Exactly why did she eagerly invite Jesus into her home?"* She had this extreme opportunity to serve Jesus and spend time with Him. Instead of getting down to the nitty gritty, she spent her time working in a vicious circle, whining about what her sister *wasn't* doing, and wasting valuable time. I want to *believe* that there was some level of purity in Martha's actions. I want to *hope* she had a desire, deep down inside to express her love for Jesus through service. But, Scripture is pretty clear concerning Jesus' reaction to Martha's somewhat sassy demand:

> "Martha, Martha, you are worried and bothered about
> so many things; but only one thing is necessary for
> which Mary has chosen the good part, which shall not
> be taken away from her." Luke 10:41-42 (NASB)

The greatest lesson I have learned from Martha is that her instinct to serve wasn't necessarily wrong; however, her motivation and attitude were flawed. She wanted recognition and pity from Jesus. Martha wanted Jesus to force her sister to do as much work as she was doing. What matters most to me when I am serving? It is the satisfaction and contentment of the ones I'm serving, and how my actions please God. When all of the cookies have melted in their mouths and only crumbs remain of the chocolate cake, I pray that the sweetness remaining with them are my smile, my graciousness, my sacrifice, and an obsession for my sweet treats . . . always coming back for more! I pray that God consistently finds me to be a good and faithful servant—a positive steward of my talents and gifts as he did the servant in Matthew 25:21 (NASB):

"His master said to him, 'Well done, good and faithful slave. You were faithful with a few things, I will put you in charge of many things; enter into the joy of your master.'"

Pizza Mix-Up

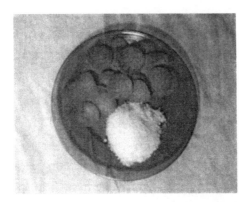

When I was young, I loved spending the night with my grandparents. Food defined my visits with them—*crème horns, cornbread, macaroni & milk, yellow cake with chocolate sauce.* Thinking about all of it makes my mouth water. When I turned 8, my mammaw decided that I should cook supper for her and my pappaw. We went to IGA and debated on what I could make (on my own) for supper. We finally decided on a Chef BOY-AR-DEE pizza kit. Should be simple . . . ingredients included, directions on the box.

There I stood in mammaw's sacred kitchen with a baking sheet and Chef BOY-AR-DEE pizza mix. I was excited, but nervous. I really wasn't sure about making the pizza without any help. I opened the box and was quickly overwhelmed with the pouch of dough mix, can of pizza sauce, and packet of parmesan cheese. For the longest time, I stood and stared at everything from the pizza kit. I knew that I needed water and oil, but what was I supposed to mix the water and oil with? No doubt, the pizza should already be in the oven. So, I did the only thing I could think of. I pulled the glass bowl close to me and proceeded to empty the pouch of dough mix, the can of pizza sauce, the packet of parmesan cheese, the water, and the oil. I slowly stirred the concoction. It didn't look like my mom's pizza and I fought back tears as I realized I couldn't figure out what I had done wrong. I quickly pressed the pizza onto the pan—nice and flat and stuck it in the oven. And then I waited. I waited until my pappaw came and removed it from the oven for me. He smiled, patted me on the head, and got me a cold bottle of Coca-Cola and a straw. We sat down at the table and ate every single bite of that pizza. My grandparents told me that it was the best pizza they had ever eaten.

Directions. I obviously didn't pay too much attention to the directions on the pizza box. I have started thinking that I tend to ignore directions in other areas of my life as well. Life is hard and I often try to figure everything out on my own—navigate the waters alone—bake up my own destiny. I need to wake up and smell the pizza sauce! God provided me with a perfect set of directions to make it through life's most difficult times. The Bible . . . a set of directions.

> "Make me know Your ways, O LORD; teach me Your
> paths. Lead me in Your truth and teach me. For You
> are the God of my salvation; for You I wait all the day."
> Psalm 25:4-5 (NASB)

If I follow those directions, I will receive wisdom and blessings from a great God. With the Bible in my hand, I always have access to the right ingredients and I can give my best effort to be successful. If and when I do panic, God comforts me and works everything for the good.

> "And we know that God causes all things to work
> together for good to those who love God, to those
> who are the called according to His purpose."
> Romans 8:28 (NASB)

God sees my mix-ups, but more than that, I think God sees my heart. He knows that I love His Word and I want to please Him and serve Him. In the same way, I'm sure my grandparents saw my pizza mix-up. However, they never laughed at me, criticized me, or embarrassed me. They called everyone they knew and told them about the best pizza they had ever eaten! My grandparents saw my heart . . . my passion to serve them and I love them dearly for giving me one of my first cooking experiences!

HIS Race!

Pounding heart, sweating palms, racing pulse—all indicators of a true competition. The only question at this point is who will win and how they will win. I do not like to lose, but what can a person do? By far, I have found myself in the loser's pit more often than the winner's circle.

It's amazing to me how often I see competition rear up in situations around me. I was a passenger in a car a few nights ago and every time we approached a stop light, the driver said, *"Alright, I'm going to beat the car in the other lane and move in and cut them off."* I laughed on the inside thinking that his intentions were rather childish . . . someone his age needing to beat the car in the other lane? Finally, I questioned why he had this urge to win. His reply was interesting. He smiled and said, *"Well, I guess it's for the same reason you wanted to beat me down the bypass last Friday night."* Ouch! He was right. We both pulled out and headed down the road. However, he was in a sports car and I was in a crossover. Every bone in my body wanted to beat him down that road and go just enough faster than him to call myself the winner.

If I'm really into a competition—water baseball with my nieces and nephews, music trivia with a friend, holiday word searches, I do not allow *anything* to cloud my vision. I'm focused . . . fixed . . . fascinated. This makes me pause to think about how competitively ambitious I am when it comes to living the Christian life. How passionately do I embrace Hebrews 12:1b (NASB)? ". . . let us also lay aside every encumbrance and the sin which so easily entangles us, and let us run with endurance the race that is set before us."

I am quick to make excuses when it comes to giving up my desires and plunging into service and ministry head-first. I allow the demons of *worry, low self-esteem,* and *fear of failure* to weigh me down and render me completely ineffective. Sins become larger than me and I fall victim to the swallowing shadows. In these instances, I'm not running *toward* something, I'm running *away* from something. It's obvious that I do not have the hunger or the willpower to win.

There is no better race to run than the one which the Lord has set before me. It is His race which builds character and integrity in the believer. It is His race which sets the soul on fire. It is His race which encourages love, forgiveness, and understanding. It is His race which eliminates the demons and sin which battle to destroy me. It is His race which offers the greatest prize of all—eternal security. He promised that, and He is waiting to come back and take me home:

> "In my Father's house are many dwelling places; if it
> were not so, I would have told you; for I go to prepare
> a place for you. If I go and prepare a place for you, I
> will come again, and receive you to Myself, that where
> I am, there you may be also." John 14:2-3 (NASB)

Pass the Sugar, Please!

"For we are His workmanship, created in Christ Jesus
for good works." Ephesians 2:10a (NASB)

I went to Kroger the other day with a plan. I had my list,
my timeline, and my journey mapped out. We are having Vacation
Bible School this week and I was picking up supplies to make
yummy treats for the adult workers. I skipped unnecessary aisles
and dodged some people that would slow me down and I felt
pretty well perfect—a textbook grocery experience. Nothing or
no one was going to break my stride!

I was completely immersed in the vanilla wafer choices . . .
mini, reduced fat, Nabisco, Keebler, etc. My mind was dancing at the
thought of people gobbling up the banana pudding I was going to
make. I knew in my heart that it would be the "hit of the night."
Just as I made my crucial choice, someone dared to say, "Excuse
me . . ." Privately, I thought, "Are you kidding me? I'm busy and
now I'm going to have to stop and talk to someone." With my
"whatever!" attitude, I pivoted and my heart turned a somersault.

Standing before me was a precious elderly gentleman. His eyes were twinkling and the last thing he was thinking about was getting out of there quickly. I could tell that he had all the time in the world, and now he was going to dip into my time. He said, *"You look like you know a lot about baking. Come over here with me."* As if hypnotized, I obediently followed him to the baking aisle. He explained to me that he had a list and just couldn't handle finding all of the items. He didn't ask me to find one item, he asked me to fill the entire list—no less than 12 items. Somewhere between the vanilla extract and the butter flavored Crisco, my focus shifted from what a hurry I had been in to what exactly this man was planning to bake.

Come to find out, the smallest ingredient in this encounter was finding out what he was going to bake. Turns out, I had two lessons to learn that morning. After his grocery basket was bulging, he invited me to the canned cooking spray section. He proceeded to tell me the best way to make popcorn and exactly which spray to use so it tastes just like *"genuine movie theatre popcorn!"* Carefully, he outlined the steps of popping fresh popcorn, laying it out in a single layer and spraying it generously with the butter flavored cooking spray. He literally put a can in *my* basket.

Nearly twenty minutes later, he turned to me with tears in his eyes. He pulled out his wallet and said he was going to pay me $5 for helping him. Of course, I refused. The man went on to say that he didn't expect anyone to do anything free for him. I realized that the absence of genuine kindness in our society is in fact a festering problem. The idea of getting paid to carry out a good work made me very sad. Furthermore, it disturbed me that he had possibly gotten the impression that he had bothered me or that I expected something in return.

Consequently, this unexpected meeting reignited a long lost fire in my heart. The fire of honest servanthood—doing good because it is what I'm called to do. It does not involve doing good only when it is convenient or when I get some kind of return for it. Indeed, it is seeing someone in need and placing myself in their path to serve . . . with an extra serving of sugar on top!

The Icing on the Cake

"Every good thing given and every perfect gift is from
above, and comes down from the Father of lights, with
whom there is no variation or shifting shadow."
James 1:17 (NASB)

I looked forward to my birthday party every year. Not because
of the gifts I would receive, but because it was the one time each
year that I got to choose the dessert that would be served. I always
wanted a bakery cake with butter cream icing. The cake was topped
off with ballerinas in pink and silver tutus. My favorite part was the
icing—it was the crowning glory of the cake and literally melted
in my mouth. It is almost embarrassing to admit how very much I
love icing even to this day.

My grandmother referred to anything special or above and
beyond normal as "*the icing on the cake.*" I got to drink coffee and
eat crème horns at her house, which totally blew my typical glass
of Tang and bowl of Froot Loops out of the water! My summer

was complete when my family made our annual 4ᵗʰ of July trip to the Irvington Drive-In. We took our big fluffy blankets and loaded in the station wagon. Of course we were excited about the movie, but the real anticipation was the fireworks! I can recall hundreds of *"icing on the cake"* moments from my childhood. These are the moments that I hold on to and cherish.

Some of my favorite *"icing on the cake"* moments now are: *hugs, chocolate cupcakes with chocolate icing, fresh flowers, kids writing a paragraph for the first time, frosty windows, unexpected dinners with a friend, surprises—any kind, conversations with my sisters, 'I love you' from my parents, cotton candy cloud days, stormy nights, remembering something I thought I had forgotten, movies at the theatre, hearing a favorite song, Eskimo kisses, a cardinal sitting in a tree, Suzy Q's and chocolate milk, bare trees in the winter, hot chocolate chip cookies, star gazing, smelling brown sugar and vanilla extract, and finding a common bond with a stranger.*

If I were to choose the number one *"icing on the cake"* memory, it would be the presence of my nieces and nephews in my life. Oh, how they have changed my perspective and motivation to get up and live life to the fullest. Technically, they are the cake, the icing, and the glass of Vitamin D milk. If I happened to never be blessed again in this life, I can say that I have within them the truest treasures God can give.

> "Behold, children are a gift of the LORD; the fruit of
> the womb is a reward." Psalm 127:3 (NASB)

We all have moments—different moments from the past and present which make us unique. As an adult, I believe I seek out special moments more than ever. I want something to cling to and hide in my heart. I believe that all of these moments—childhood and adult are *all* made possible by God. Everything I have or am allowed to enjoy comes straight from heaven. Day after day, God just decides to bless me. Even if another person brings the moment to reality, it started out in God's heart because He knew me . . . and He knew that I would love it.

I Shall Not Be Moved

"He will be like a tree firmly planted by streams of
water, which yields its fruit in its season and its leaf
does not wither; and in whatever he does, he prospers."
Psalm 1:3 (NASB)

I learned all kinds of catchy songs as a child. Among my
favorites were *Father Abraham, Joy, Joy, Joy Down in My Heart, Deep
and Wide, and Jesus Loves Me.* The tunes still ripple through the
fibers of my soul and the words are forever trapped in my heart.
These songs served as some of life's greatest lessons for me. Today I
was thinking about the song, *I Shall Not Be Moved.* The following
lyrics were based on Psalm 10:6 (NASB), "He says to himself, 'I
will not be moved.'"

I shall not be, I shall not be moved.
I shall not be, I shall not be moved.
Like a tree planted by the water.
I shall not be moved.

All trees have distinct characteristics which make them appealing and beautiful. Take for instance, the glorious sassafras tree. This tree stands out for a variety of reasons. First, it has an intoxicating, pleasant fragrance. The sweet odor invites wildlife to eat from it and bask in the comfort of its shade. Second, the tree bears three different shaped leaves, making it interesting and unique. Because of the leaf formations, the tree is popular and easy to identify. Finally, the sassafras tree is deeply rooted in the richness of the earth giving it strength and longevity.

There is an uncanny connection between a sassafras tree and a believer. Christ calls on and expects us to carry His Good News to everyone. 2 Corinthians 2:14b-15 (NASB) says,

"But thanks be to God, who always leads us in triumph
in Christ, and manifests through us the sweet aroma
of the knowledge of Him in every place. For we are a
fragrance of Christ to God among those who are being
saved and among those who are perishing."

I have to ask myself quite frequently what message I'm sending to the world around me. Carefully, I must consider how my actions, character traits, speech, and decisions affect others. Hopefully, I do not omit the odors of a bitter spirit, sour attitude, or rotten personality. If so, people will immediately be turned off and search elsewhere to find someone to spend time with. Someone that smells . . . well, yummy!

Living in this dark and lonely world, it is more important than ever for us to stand out as genuine followers of Christ. If we are no different than the rest of the world, we will simply blend in and become complacent. The world will be able to identify each of us by the fruit we bear as outlined in Galatians 5:22-23 (NASB):

"But the fruit of the Spirit is love, joy, peace, patience,
kindness, goodness, faithfulness, gentleness, self-control;
against such things there is no law."

The fruit we bear will be an indicator of our life in Christ and the unique character He builds in each of us. Despite popular belief, godly character is attractive and draws others closer. The moment we give our lives to Christ, our roots are anchored in the fertile soil of Him. He nurtures us by giving us Living Water and the Bread of Life. We are equipped to handle the things that life throws at us—coming out on the other side of trials and tribulations with more perseverance and grace. Life in Christ means that we can grow into beautiful servants and never be moved from His presence.

White Rabbit Syndrome

One of my favorite pastimes is people watching. Based on what I see and hear, I sum people up and attempt to imagine their story. Observations are made and conclusions are drawn whether they are right or not. If someone else saw the same person, they would detect a different story.

Recently, I spent several hours waiting for flights at the airport. The airport is a metropolis of rushing bodies coming and going from one destination to the next. It's as if people are chanting the words of the White Rabbit from *Alice in Wonderland*, "*I'm late, I'm late for a very important date!!*" The gates were bustling and Starbucks was brewing as person after person crossed my path. Some took a seat, others stood and pondered, and others passed right on by. Unofficially, I came across jilted lovers, honest businessmen, dishonest spouses, grieving souls, unwanted children, vacationers with a rendezvous in another city, family members looking forward to a reunion, runners—young and old trying to escape, and searchers . . . just looking for something new under the sun. Some had round trip tickets and others had a one way ticket to a new life.

Something stirred inside me with each different person. Indeed, we were crossing paths. Was God giving me a two hour layover for a reason? Was He creating a little timetable for me to make a difference in someone else's life? Even with this realization, I would consciously avoid eye contact and feel uncomfortable. There were a few I wanted to strike up a conversation with, but didn't. Still, there were others that I hoped didn't talk to me. For some reason, they disturbed me and I found myself making that infamous pact with God: *Dear God, please take these people away and I will do everything else you ever ask me to do . . . . even if I don't have time, I'll do everything!* This trip hadn't been intended for evangelism. So, I was going to sit right there in that airport and listen to my IPod—that was my plan! I was using my time in my own way by hook or by crook.

The thing that was true about each and every person is the fact that they all really did have a story and it should have been of utmost importance for me to listen to them. It is possible they would have allowed me to dig deeper and even surprise them by sharing something of worth to add to their story.

When I allow time to dictate whether I interact with someone or avoid them, I allow an eternally significant moment to pass through my fingertips. Shame on me! In Matthew 28:19-20 (NASB), Jesus commanded:

> "Go therefore and make disciples of all nations,
> baptizing them in the name of the Father and of the
> Son and of the Holy Spirit, teaching them to observe
> all that I commanded you; and lo, I am with you
> always, even to the end of the age."

This statement is famously called the Great Commission—one of Jesus' final commands to His disciples. But, the command was not only intended for those men who stood before Him on that day. Am I not a disciple? If so, it was intended to echo through the ages and become a part of my spiritual walk right here today. This should be the heartbeat of every believer. The Great Commission. A command not merely a suggestion.

69

Deep Fried Obsession

Within a two day period, two people basically referred to me as "obsessed." Something inside me snapped and I thought to myself, "No way! Obsession is how you describe people who cannot control what they do or say!"

The first person referred to me as obsessed because I wanted to be in control of getting something done. I was in town for a limited time and I had a tally in my mind of what I wanted to accomplish. Leaving without taking care of it wasn't an option. Although the promise was made that she would "take care" of getting it done for me, it wasn't enough. I felt the urgent necessity to see it through from start to finish—on my own. Here is what I obviously believed to be true at the time. She wouldn't do it fast enough. She might not get it done. She wouldn't do it *my way*. Whatever my reasoning, I came across as obsessed. She was amused rather than offended and we shared a good laugh!

I went to dinner with a friend a few nights ago. Since I had just returned from a trip, I had quite an adventure to share. He wanted to listen and even encouraged me to tell him everything. During an entire dinner, I only shared a fraction of what I wanted to because I was so enthralled with getting it just right. Detail after flowery detail abounded, but I got to the final morsel of information and realized I hadn't really told him anything of value. I had missed the meat—what he really wanted to know. On the way home, he told me that I am obsessed with details and he would be happy to just get the punch line. His constructive criticism was peppered with humor and I proceeded to practice answering his questions without the "fluff." Him: "*What did you eat for lunch?*" Me: "*Turkey.*" Him: "*What are you doing tomorrow?*" Me: "*Meeting.*" Him: "*Are you glad to be home?*" Me: "*Yes.*" It was nearly impossible not to add that the turkey sandwich came from Subway where I ran into a friend. I would have liked to add that Subway is always out of spinach and the tomatoes were more white than red. Oh, and by the way, they were out of my favorite chips! Details bubbled up inside me and it was painful to give one word answers!

Now that I have been labeled by two people who have never spoken to each other, I am ready and willing to admit that I am no doubt, obsessed. I am obsessed with control and details. The real question is whether obsession is healthy or not. Were obsession a meal, would it look like fried chicken and all the fixings or would it better resemble a crispy veggie salad served with a side of fat free vinaigrette? I must take into consideration how I feel after the obsessive episode. Does it leave my brain feeling bloated and chubby? Sadly, yes.

I believe the root of my obsession is worry and insecurity. And as a believer, I understand that this kind of attitude not only destroys my quality of life, but is not appealing to God. After all, He did promise to take care of me in any and all circumstances.

"And my God will supply all your needs according
to his riches in glory in Christ Jesus."
Philippians 4:19 (NASB)

If I spend my time obsessing over control and details, I miss out on many of life's simple blessings. My plan is to let God obsess over me and the particulars in my life. If He is going to supply all of my needs then my life will be overflowing with His love. My heart will be filled with God and good things and my obsessive nature will slowly fade.

My Comfort

"Hear, my son, to your father's instruction and do
not forsake your mother's teaching; indeed they are
a graceful wreath to your head and ornaments about
your neck." Proverbs 1:8-9 (NASB)

Few things can compare to the feeling of being safe and sound. As a teacher, I see children who go to bed hungry, come to school dirty, and live life full of fear and disappointment. Some children never know what it feels like to eat a home cooked meal. They have never experienced the comfort of a nice, warm bath with soap to wash their body. Rather than thinking about riding bikes and climbing trees, they are thinking about where to hide when daddy gets home or what not to tell the teachers about *last night*. I count myself blessed to have lived a life that leaves me feeling safe and sound.

My dad tucked me in bed at night. I would brush my teeth and climb in the bed next to my sister and we would wait . . . wait for him to saunter down the hallway and into our bedroom. He would find us with our legs and bare feet stretched out across the crisp, white sheet. He would assure us that no one was looking in the windows or hiding under our bed, pull the quilt up to our chins, kiss us on the forehead, and turn out the light. As he left the room, he said, "*Go to sleep now, girls. I love you.*" This was a ritual and became the greatest source of comfort I have ever experienced. I was secure in the fact that my dad loved me because he told me every single day.

My mom never worked outside the home. She was there when we left for school and she was there when we returned home. My mom washed our clothes and worked hard to make us feel extra special. My sisters and I would leap off the bus and rush to the house because we had missed her so much! Before we landed on the front door, the smell of chocolate chip snack cake danced from the kitchen straight to our noses. It was a sweet comfort just knowing she was there and all was well. I knew I was safe because my mom spent every waking moment protecting me.

Indeed my parents gave me the gifts of comfort, love, and protection. Not only did I experience these great gifts, but they taught me how to extend comfort, love, and protection to other people. I believe that God placed a man and woman of great character in my life so that I could use what they taught me to enhance the lives of the people in my path.

My great prayer is that God would save all the children from heartache and sadness. I pray that the angel of the Lord would encamp around suffering children and give them a sense of safety:

> "The angel of the LORD encamps around those who
> fear Him, and rescues them." Psalm 34:7 (NASB)

May God use me each and every day in my classroom and the world to demonstrate comfort, love, and protection. I realize now that what my family had was rare—something that others hunger and thirst after. I thank God for my dad and mom . . . my comfort.

Kaleidoscope

I was so excited when my mom let us buy a kaleidoscope at Park's where we shopped on Saturday afternoons. It was one of my favorite toys ever! I'm pretty sure I didn't share well with my sisters. I would sit for hours and slowly turn the kaleidoscope and experience the wonders of color and design. What could be seen with each turn is unique and beautiful.

I hadn't had a kaleidoscope for years and years, but I truly believed that I would receive as much enjoyment now from one as I did in my childhood. My former youth leader is an extremely keen listener. She has heard me talk about loving kaleidoscopes. I was nearly speechless when I received an early Christmas gift from her and I found inside a beautiful kaleidoscope. I cannot tell you how many moments I have spent "playing."

When I consider the make-up of the kaleidoscope, I am curious about how the colorful pieces stay in place and create logical, intricate patterns. Another person could take the same kaleidoscope and the fancywork they observe would be unlike what I see. Things would catch their eye that I didn't even notice. Colors would stand out that I never detected. The designs would be perceived in vastly different ways.

I was reminded of the diversity of a kaleidoscope during a recent conversation about *"who people think I am."* Time and circumstances carry us into many relationships. Daughter, sister, aunt, granddaughter, cousin, friend, and teacher. Beyond the core relationship, these people would describe me using many a myriad of adjectives and character traits. The people I am closest to see things in me that they love and are drawn to. Sometimes, they point out qualities in me that I have never thought about—*strong spirit, tender heart, sassy* ...This is because they all see me through a different set of eyes under varying circumstances. Above all, God placed me here on earth to touch the lives of other individuals. Those individuals should be honored and encouraged:

"Do not merely look out for your own interests, but
also for the interests of others." Philippians 2:4 (NASB)

"Be devoted to another in brotherly love; give
preference to one another in honor."
Romans 12:10 (NASB)

Reliving Memories

"Memory is a way of holding onto the things you love,
the things you are, the things you never want to lose."
~Kevin Arnold, The Wonder Years

I am a memory keeper. Memories embody everything that is special and sacred to me. I am a complex package tied up with memories—all kinds of memories. These memories are the ribbons running through my mind revealing the person I have become.

My oldest memory is of being at the funeral home when my grandmother died. I was just shy of 2 years old. The room where her casket rested was cavernous and icy cold. The carpet was peppered with cabbage roses and it was eerily quiet. I can still picture Wilma Grace Pollock lying there void of life. She didn't reach up and pinch my cheeks, and she didn't wink at me with her mischievous eyes. Tucked in her hands was a bouquet of four tiny roses—one for each granddaughter. I towered above her; perched on my daddy's arm. This memory reminds me of sweet, unconditional love of I Peter 1:22b (NASB):

"Fervently love one another from the heart."

When I was 4 years old, I climbed on my grandmother's chest freezer for an unknown reason. The mystery unraveled as my mother and aunt tried to figure out how I had managed such a feat. There was nothing close enough to the freezer for me to climb on; so I apparently scaled the slippery freezer under my own power. I do not remember getting there, but I remember *being* there. Sitting gloriously high on my mountain, I heard my aunt cry out, "Karen Beth! What in the world are you doing up there?" This memory reminds me of uninhibited, valiant courage described in Psalm 31:24 (NASB):

"Be strong and let your heart take courage, all you who
hope in the Lord."

I learned to roller-skate at a 1950's roller rink with a wavy, wooden floor. The rails were treacherously loose and offered little in the way of security. I skated rapidly around and around the little rink. The curves were my favorite! Eventually, I managed to skate backwards and could be the head or tail of the whip.

I took my students on a field trip. I knew that the destination offered roller-skating as an activity, but I never planned on indulging. My students started asking me to skate with them and the memories flooded back. Fun-loving freedom stood out the most in my mind. As I watched from the sidelines, one child after another glided past me—making new memories of their own. Their young, limber moves made it look like a piece of cake. I was somewhat jealous. I silently wondered, "Could I relive the memory?" "Is it possible to time travel back to 1987 and pick up where I left off?" Finally, my curiosity won out and I snuck over to the skate counter. I laced up my roller skates and cautiously made my way to the entrance of the rink. My legs felt like Jell-o and the strobe lights made me dizzy. Almost instantly, I realized that my skating skills had gotten just a tad bit rusty. My students were guardian angels—they wanted to hold my hand, teach me to use the brakes, and rescue me when I . . . *fell!*

Needless to say, roller-skating did not come back to me like I believed it might. I never let go of the rail, I couldn't remember how to move my feet, and crawling to the wall to gain my composure was just a little embarrassing. However, a few things remained the same. It was flat out fun!! It was challenging in a good way. It made me thankful and glad that God has given me such a devoted memory. My 3rd grade students taught me a great lesson that day. It actually is possible to bring a memory back to the surface and experience some of the same familiar feelings. And that is the beautiful thing about memories—pleasant or unpleasant, we deal with them each and every day. They become what we fondly refer to as *our story*.

The Bare Naked Truth

We are at our most innocent when we are born—*naked, defenseless, dependent, sinless*. Babies have nothing to hide and they have no shame. Their feelings and emotions are fully exposed and there is nothing they can do about it. Babies are the real deal! They are incapable of being anything other than perfect. Everything they do is sweet and precious and priceless.

Somewhere between birth and growing up, we develop the urge to do things like "hide," "cover up," and "feel ashamed." Most of our life is spent playing peek-a-boo with God and the world. We wonder, "*Who heard me?*" "*Who saw me?*" "*Who knows what I really am deep down inside?*" We allow the circumstances of life to light our way, and we decide to start making decisions on our own ... some good and some bad. No longer are we satisfied to have our human needs met, we want our *desires* met. We make weak decisions, treat others with disrespect, and misrepresent who we are in Christ. It is downright embarrassing what we will do to get what we want. We suddenly forget things like honesty, integrity, and love. Ignoring the value of other people, our goodness disappears and we are trapped in a cycle of dishonor and selfishness.

As long as we are getting by with sinning, we feel pretty successful about ourselves. We move along and never consider the consequences. At least, not until we are exposed. You probably remember our good friends Adam and Eve. God created them and they didn't require a stitch of clothing! They were happy and content. Although they gallivanted about the garden naked, they "were not ashamed" (Genesis 2:25 NASB). The moment sin entered their lives, they were aware of their bare nakedness—and they "were ashamed" (Genesis 3:7 NASB). Is it the peaceful communion with one another and God that we remember most about Adam and Eve or is it their transgression? The serpent, the tree, the *apple*? One of the Bible's most fascinating blame games has captivated readers for centuries, and it is in fact the SIN which stirs in our mind.

While we are busy camouflaging ourselves, God is looking for us to fulfill His will, live in harmony with people, and love. He wants us to be ready, willing, and able to do whatever He asks us to do. In our hiding place, we wallow in our pity and convince ourselves that we are unworthy to serve a great and mighty God. In our solitary confinement, we assume that God won't find us. What a great plan! Hiding from God. It doesn't take long for Him to find us. Psalm 139:7-10 (NASB) paints a beautiful picture of what hide and seek with God looks like.

"Where can I go from Your Spirit?
Or where can I flee from Your presence?
If I ascend to heaven, You are there;
If I make my bed in Sheol, behold, You are there.
If I take the wings of the dawn,
If I dwell in the remotest part of the sea,
Even there Your hand will lead me;
And Your right hand will lay hold of me."

Someone once said, "It is our light, not our darkness that most frightens us." When we find ourselves in the midst of a Garden of Eden experience, a choice must be made. Continue on and allow the heart to grow darker and darker until it reflects the shadows of night or accept forgiveness from God and allow Him to purify the heart until it illuminates the True Light.

Royalty

"I am a princess. All girls are."
—Sara (The Little Princess)

The royal family is intriguing to me. To be perfectly honest, they are *extremely* intriguing to me. I became a royal follower when Diana entered the scene. I was there when she said, "I do." I watched the ceremony on television and then turned around and bought all of the magazines that featured pictures. When a book was published, I went to the public library, brought it home, and read it from cover to cover. The entire event sparked an interest in me for all things royal. Recently, William and Kate were married. I woke up at 4 a.m. to watch the festivities. I didn't want to miss William leaving the castle. I was anxious to get that first glimpse of Kate's wedding gown. I didn't want to miss the kiss on the balcony. This time, it prompted me to think about what was in store for me and my "happily ever after."

You may be asking why I would be so intrigued. It isn't the money, material possessions, or servants. It isn't the jewels, bodyguards, or prestige. It really comes down to security and being set apart. As a princess, someone is always in your corner—watching over you, protecting you, and wanting the best for you. When you are a princess, you know and understand what is expected of you—your purpose is set out before you, and you live to meet or exceed those expectations.

I realize that I cannot simply "wish upon a star" and change my position in this life. Webster defines royalty as, *"Belonging to an elite class; of noble character."* While my family is the best in the world, we are not elite and we are not from nobility. Diana and Kate were both commoners who happened upon a prince. The chances of meeting a real live prince are nearly impossible. While I understand they do exist, I just don't believe I'm going to run into a prince. After drawing these conclusions, shouldn't I just forget the whole idea and move on with my present reality? Do I give up and accept the theory that a road to royalty does not exist for me?

Sara from the *Little Princess* said, "I am a princess. All girls are. Even if they live in tiny, old attics, even if they dress in rags, even if they aren't pretty, or smart, or young. They're still princesses. All of us." Sara's statement gave me a glimmer of hope because I actually fit most of her princess profile. It encouraged me to examine what God's Word has to say about my royal status. Romans 8:17 (NASB) says,

> "And if children, heirs also—heirs of God and fellow
> heirs with Christ, if indeed we suffer with Him so that
> we may be glorified with Him."

I fell in love with Jesus years and years ago. He has been a constant in my life; giving me the sense of security that I need. Jesus is always on my side and he wraps me in His robes of righteousness. My heart is not my own for it belongs to the King of kings. His Word is a scepter in my hand. A diamond tiara adorns my head where He wore a crown of thorns. Through His death, I have entered into a royal family that carries the promise of eternal life. Earthly kings and kingdoms will pass away, but His Kingdom is everlasting. As I endure this life and walk daily on a path that is not always easy, I can turn my face toward heaven and feel the glory and splendor that belong only to the children—the princes and princesses of the King.

Mud Pies and Chocolate Chip Cookies

"Be hospitable to one another without complaint.
As each one has received a special gift, employ it in
serving one another as good stewards of the manifold
grace of God." 1 Peter 4:9-10 (NASB)

In thinking about my childhood, I wonder exactly what impacted the strength of my servant's heart. What did I enjoy playing as a child? What talents did I try to foster? What activities brought delight to my afternoons? Suddenly, memories started flooding my mind, and they all had a common theme: hospitality.

Running a restaurant, building a house outlined with sticks, or baking mud pies . . . those were usually my choices when I got to pick what we were going to play. One summer, my sisters and I decided to open a mud pie bakery. The basement was literally filled with extravagant mud pies. We used red clay, potting soil, and regular old dirt to make different types of chocolate. To mold the pies, we used various containers—even some forbidden ones from my mother's kitchen. The finishing touches were fluffy yellow dandelions, tender blades of grass, velvety rose petals, plump pebbles, and golden acorns. Each pie was unique and loaded with tender loving care. If you tried real hard, you could smell the gooey sweets all the way up and down our road. Wonderfully colorful customers paid top prices for our pies. News spread far and wide about the tiny bakery in the basement. Of course, the customers were imaginary, but believing they had certain expectations gave me the desire to make people happy by cooking for them.

One of the first real desserts I learned to make was fried pies. I learned from my mom, and my motivation was seeing my dad smile. My grandmother had made fried pies for him all his life. I put everything into rolling out the dough, filling the pies, and frying them to perfect crispiness. My proudest moments were when he bit into the pie and the yummy filling popped out the sides; declaring their goodness. I quickly learned that I could capture his heart with banana pudding, coconut pie, and yellow cake with chocolate frosting.

Over the past couple of years, my servant heart and baking heart have collided. I have realized that I can use my gift of hospitality and baking to touch the lives of the people God places in my life. Time spent baking a batch of chocolate chip cookies for a best friend is so worth it when I know it makes them feel special. Words can't express what I feel when a grieving family enjoys a homemade chocolate cake at the funeral dinner of their loved one. My nieces and nephews make my day when they make requests for my specialties.

When you can reach out to someone with a homemade treat, it proves how important they are in your life. When I use this heavenly gift, I feel closer to God and I thank Him for teaching me lessons about hospitality throughout my life. Lessons of hospitality that began in the old days at the mud pie bakery.

Nosey Rosey

When I was 12 years old, my favorite grandfather passed away. As I sat beside my youth leader, I asked, "Why did he have to die?" She replied, "God was ready for him to be in heaven." That was a good answer and it made sense. At least it was as good as any answer that an adult could have given me. I was scared that God might want me in heaven sometime soon.

As if elementary school wasn't tough enough, my aunt and uncle decided to get a divorce. As I sat beside my aunt, I asked, "Why did Uncle Dennis leave?" She said, "He doesn't love me anymore." I wondered if he had stopped loving me, too.

When I first understood about child abuse, I was in middle school. My mom was on jury duty and the person on trial was being accused of abusing their child. As I sat beside my mother, I asked, "Why did that mom hit her child?" She replied, "She is full of anger and cannot control herself." I was glad she wasn't my mother.

True shock set in my first year of college when I heard about a girl being raped. I was naive, but I figured out what it meant.

As I sat beside my sister, I asked, "Why would a man do that to a woman?" She replied, "They think they need to control other people and women are easy targets." I understood that I was a target, too.

I'm a teacher now and one of the most difficult challenges I face is answering those tough questions about life. In my earliest years of teaching, one of my students lost his uncle—his hero. As I tried to minister to him, I realized that I didn't have very many answers. The ones that I did provide were weak at best. He would look at me with those doubtful eyes and I knew he believed that I absolutely had no clue what the right answers really were. His most poignant question was, *"Why did God need a farmer in heaven? He was only 26 years old."* I wonder if my student considers whether he might die when he's 26 years old.

I am what they call in the education field an "existentialist." I fight to know the answer to all of life's burning questions. I question and research . . . question and research . . . question and research. The world's answer to my questions is, *"Just Google it!"* Google is actually pretty amazing. A wealth of knowledge is housed there in bits and bytes. It has answered many questions for me. Sure Google is great for figuring out whether or not "ain't" is a real word and what kind of doctor takes care of certain ailments. However, Google has not satisfied my curiosity on some questions—*why do bad things happen to good people* or *why does death visit some people at an early age?* The quizzical question mark lurks in the corner of my mind—taunting and teasing me into frustration. Google just doesn't get it; so I look elsewhere.

Long before encyclopedias were written and Google was a household name, God was thinking about what a Nosey Rosey I would be. He knew that I would have questions and seek to find the answers. He knew that I would need for things to make sense and that I would require closure. Being the wonderful Father that He is, He went to work in the lives of some great men of faith. Through these men, He fashioned what would be the bestseller of all time—a gift full of mystery, drama, love, suspense, poetry, parables, promises, and peril. He is the greatest Author ever and

His book is called the Holy Bible. The words found there can be trusted and they never lie—It is the Truth: "All Scripture is inspired by God and profitable for teaching, for reproof, for correction, for training in righteousness." 2 Timothy 3:16 (NASB)

Tick and Tock: The Twins of Time

"There is an appointed time for everything. And there
is a time for every event under heaven."
Ecclesiastes 3:1 (NASB)

We wake up each morning and instantly encounter the arch
enemy—time. Clocks and watches glare at us with their gnashing
teeth and dare us to slip into battle with them. Tick and Tock
remind us that we *will* acknowledge them as supreme or be left in
the dust. After all, the twins have already won the following wars:
Late and You Know It, You Blew Another Deadline, and *Oh, I'm Sorry
You Totally Missed Out!* I suppose we could band together and
destroy all of the timepieces in sight and start out on a course with
unlimited time at our disposal.

If I could have control of one thing in the world, it would be
time. I would harness all of the power that time has over my life
and cast it into the depths of the ocean. I want time to see the
people that I adore and to do the things I never take the time to do.
My obsession with controlling time would not only benefit me,

but those that I love. With unlimited time, my joy would return and possibilities would be endless. The hands of time would not be able to choke me. I want quality seconds, minutes, and hours to sit down face to face with the people I count special and have a truly meaningful conversation. I could bake cakes and cookies and brownies and still have time left over to chill out. Time is darkness . . . a bottomless pit that would love to suffocate me.

My father used to have a hobby of building clocks. His workshop was brimming with lumber, wood glue, clock faces, and hands. I would sneak away from my mom sometimes and go to his workshop. When I was very young, he would let me sit on the work bench and watch him sand or stain the wood. I loved the smell of that workshop. Sometimes, he would let me hold things for him or hand him the necessary tools. He took his time because he wanted the clock to be perfect. And to no surprise, they always were perfect. My father taught me that all great things take time. He would look at me and say, *"Karen, you can't rush things. If you want it to turn out right, take your time."*

So, lately I have been thinking about asking Tick and Tock to be my friend. After all, they could probably help me out when I'm in one of my frantic races with time. If I were friends with Tick and Tock, I would better understand that they aren't really out to destroy me, but rather have my best interest at heart. Tick and Tock are actually pretty classy showing up in interesting places decked out differently each and every time. One day they may be an elegant grandfather clock encouraging me to sit and relax, the next a hip hopping stopwatch spurring me on to finish the race, and the next a sassy alarm clock daring me to sleep one minute over.

I would venture to say that the lesson I learned in that dusty workshop has become a sure and constant part of who I am. I have learned to take pride in the tasks at hand and complete them to the best of my ability. I may plan to accomplish five things on any given day, but it doesn't mean my plan is realized. As Proverbs 19:21 (NASB) states, "Many plans are in a man's heart, but the counsel of the Lord will stand," I can rush and fret, and get bent out of shape. I can even "freak out" about things, but nothing will ever change what the Lord has planned. No matter how much of my time He wants, I must submit. The earth rotates and the seas roll on His time. The seasons change and the storms rage on His time. The flower blooms and withers on His time. He alone holds the clock of my life in His mighty hands. The moment of my last breath . . . He knows. And Tick and Tock will be right there guarding my body and summoning others to, *"Spend the time you have wisely."*

Jinkies!

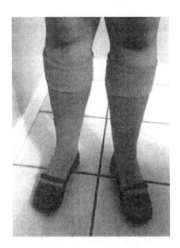

I loved cartoons and sitcoms as a child. *Scooby Doo* was definitely among my favorites. I always enjoyed the silly predicaments the "gang" found themselves in. However, the most exciting moment to me was when all of the clues came together and the mystery was solved!

The characters in *Scooby Doo* had their own special appeal and share of fans. I have friends who have compared me to the character of Velma. Now, I admit, that at first, it is a bit disheartening not to be labeled a Daphne. After all, she was known for her beauty and style. She definitely turned heads! Velma, on the other hand was quirky, nearsighted, and a little bit "thick." Yes, in the eyes of a woman, it would be much more flattering to be called Daphne. However, the Bible teaches,

> "Charm is deceitful and beauty is vain, But a woman
> who fears the LORD, she shall be praised."
> Proverbs 31:30 (NASB)

Now, I realize it isn't a sin to be beautiful—some people are blessed in that, and it can be used as much as any other gift from God. But, since I am perceived as a Velma, I decided to zero in on the qualities that make a woman like Velma godly. Velma was extremely intelligent. She had a vast knowledge of science and was sharp as a tack when it came to collecting clues and unraveling mysteries. On most occasions, Velma was the sharpest sleuth. It's amazing to me that God created us with the ability to learn to the point of infinity. Our brains can never be filled up as to not accept more information. There are tons of wonderful things to learn about in the world, but it is my desire to seal the words of God in my heart. I do not want to appear comfortably complacent to others. Rather, I yearn to draw upon sweet promises and lessons that will increase my knowledge base. Being "Bible" smart makes life bearable. It makes me a champion—a survivor. It is with honor, eagerness, and zeal that I approach the Word of God and seek His brand of wisdom.

> "But the wisdom that comes from heaven is first of all
> pure; then peace-loving, considerate, submissive, full of
> mercy and good fruit, impartial and sincere."
> James 3:17 (NASB)

It was rare for Velma not to come to across as mesmerized and surprised—filled with wonder and awe. Since Velma was in the business of cracking cases, there probably was some level of fear which helped drive her adrenaline to new heights. You would know that Velma was excited when she exclaimed, "*Jeepers, Shaggy! Take a look at that!!*" She wasn't really terrified, but she was just a little bit spooked and amazed. I feel like that sometimes when I face trials and temptations. He can punish me, discipline me, convict me, and challenge me. He alone holds the key to my beginning and my ending. That's the spooky part of Christianity. His power . . . His majesty . . . His awesomeness is overwhelming to me and I recognize that indeed He is bigger and stronger than I will ever be. That's the amazing part of Christianity. In seeking to honor God with my life, I distinguish between His place in the universe and my place. I am not *afraid* of God, but I have a reverent fear of Him. This reverence allows me to worship Him as the one true God.

> "Let all the earth fear the Lord; let all the inhabitants of
> the world stand in awe of Him." Psalm 33:8 (NASB)

Although the viewer was always led to believe that there were ghosts, goblins, witches, and monsters terrorizing first one place and then another, at the end of the mystery, the masks would come off and the criminal was actually some bitter human being. Velma could sift through the trail of terror and discover why a seemingly good person had gone bad. Typically, it boiled down to a heart that had grown cold with evil, deceit, and greed. So, Velma's motivation was to help take out the villain and restore order for everyone involved. Likewise, we know that the devil moves about; hoping to stir someone to commit a crime, destroy a life, or crush a relationship. He inhabits any willing character and glories in the path of destruction. The devil is our enemy. Hate and cruelty seep from him and poisons the hearts of man. He has no mercy! For this reason, I must be prepared—ready to fight and defend.

> "Be of sober spirit, be on the alert. Your adversary,
> the devil, prowls around like a roaring lion, seeking
> someone to devour." I Peter 5:8 (NASB)

I may never be a Daphne with flowing hair and shapely legs. A Fred may never look my way with his dreamy eyes and stylish ascot. However, I have decided that being a Velma isn't really a put-down. When I consider the full character of Velma, it's actually quite a compliment to be compared to her. I might even be inclined to say, *"Jinkies, guys! Thanks for seeing the hidden potential in me."*

When Christmas Isn't Red and Green

If you had asked me even a year ago to attach a color to the Christmas season, I would have said candy apple red or emerald green. Most people would, I believe. As I think about the color of my last Christmas, I am drawn to my childhood. My favorite outside activity was riding bikes. I had the coolest bike in the neighborhood. It was called *Strawberry Sizzler* and it had a banana seat covered in strawberries. I raced like the wind on that bike—it was my greatest treasure.

As the years passed, I abandoned my bike for other hobbies and it slowly rusted down behind my dad's garage. I no longer had a desire to work my body and pretend to travel to exotic places. I changed . . . moved on and I didn't take the bike with me. Where I had once gone on two wheels, I went on two feet.

A few months before Christmas, the wheels of my mind started turning and the spokes started spinning. I had this strange and wonderful sensation to take off unhindered on a bike again. The only thing standing between me and getting a new bike was the holidays. I knew that I had to be mature and think of others first. I couldn't possibly make a selfish purchase for myself at Christmas.

So, I researched, prayed, and waited. I started feelin' blue, but in a good way. The bike I had set my heart on was baby blue and white. Blue wasn't conjuring up feelings of sorrow or sadness, but rather smiles and happiness. I looked forward to the day I could order the bike and get healthy. I felt that as a Christian, this was a good goal for me to set since the Bible definitely encourages us to take care of our bodies:

> "Or do you not know that your body is a temple of
> the Holy Spirit who is in you, whom you have from
> God, and you are not your own? For you have been
> bought with a price: therefore glorify God in your
> body." 1 Corinthians 6:19-20 (NASB)

I told my closest family and friends what my plan was and they were all very excited for me. They agreed that it was a great idea and they supported me 100%. Their exhilaration only enhanced my anxiousness. I went so far as to show them pictures of the bike, which made it seem even more real. Sooner than later, I would discover that one particular friend had listened with a noble intent in his heart. He had paid attention and committed my dream to his memory.

For more than a month, he dropped hints about his Christmas gift for me. He was very tricky and I felt like I was on a wild goose chase. I settled in my soul to be patient and wait for Christmas Eve. The magic moment finally rolled around with the scent of peppermint candy canes and snow. I felt like a little girl when I was told to close my eyes and wait for the signal.

As I slowly opened my eyes, I was amazed to see my beautiful blue bike sitting before me. I was overcome with emotions and I found it difficult to express how I felt. In my opinion, my friend had moved heaven and earth to make me happy. Simply put, he had made my day. Although I absolutely love the bike, it wasn't the material side of the gift that brought tears to my eyes. It was the sweet sacrifice that Stephen had made for me when he could have spent his money on a hundred other things. It was the look on his face when he saw how pleased I was. It was the honest way that he had heard my wish through the jibber jabber of conversations we had shared. He had genuinely wanted to make me happy. He knew my goals for the coming year and the bike was a part of that. His friendship and kindness were a true biblical example of encouragement:

> "Therefore encourage one another and build up one
> another . . ." Thessalonians 5:11a (NASB)

> "Iron sharpens iron, so one man sharpens another."
> —Proverbs 27:17 (NASB)

The bike is my pride and joy. Every time I ride, I am reminded of my wonderful friend and his generosity. Stephen made the way for me to honor God—my Christmas was filled with merriment and I have never felt *bluer*.

No Ordinary Tree

My earliest and fondest tree memory dates back to 1978. The place to be during every season of the year was my grandparents' quaint home in a rural farming community. You couldn't call their place a real farm, but they insisted it had all the proper makings of one. In reality, my grandfather had one horse named Whiskey, a jersey cow named Jersey, and a handful of very nonproductive chickens. There was a so-called barn, but looking back now, I think it would count more as a tool shed. There was a pond as well, but it was so far back on the property it didn't really matter whether it was there or not.

On this so-called farm was a gigantic Sugar Maple tree. It was strategically located beside the tiny, white house. The tree was the first thing you saw when you drove up the driveway. As season gave way to season, the tree stood at attention, waiting for the seven grandchildren to march back in for a visit. That tree was a gift. A gift straight from God.

"Out of the ground the Lord God caused to grow
every tree that is pleasing to the sight and good for
food . . ." Genesis 2:9a (NASB)

In winter, we would stand at the windows and breathe on them so the heavy frost would melt. Sometimes we even placed our warm cheeks and hands on the frigid glass in an effort to defrost the window and catch a clear view of the tree. We had an inexplicable need to steal one quick glance at the magnificent, naked Sugar Maple that had surrendered to Mother Nature's icy grip.

Spring came, and with it, tiny buds burst forth from the crooked branches. Birds busied themselves building nests. They flew in with straw, shoestrings, and horse hair to design their mansions in the treetops. It was on those breezy spring days that I realized God's plan for trees and the part they played in creation and animal life.

As Summer tip-toed in, we would invade the rug of downy grass beneath the Sugar Maple. Leaves brought our tree full circle and we were shaded from the scorching heat. We'd tell stories, and make plans to strip the nearby grapevines of their precious fruit. We ate fresh grapes and drank sweet tea under the tree. It was our meeting place—the spot where reality melted into fantasy.

Fall blew in and the Sugar Maple slowly undressed. We would wildly pile the leaves into huge mountains and dare each other to jump in face first. It was comical to watch the squirrels scurry around to gather their winter supply of acorns and various other nuts. The tree became their storehouse and they were proud with their bushy tails held high. As God blessed us with the beauty of the seasons, our memories were etched with the sounds, sights, and smells of that place.

"There is an appointed time for everything. And there
is a time for every event under heaven."
Ecclesiastes 3:1 (NASB)

Although the tree underwent changes with the seasons, one thing remained the same. There was an enormous exposed root that jutted out from the front of the tree. Within the root was a pearl—a treasure! Well, it wasn't an actual pearl, but it definitely looked like one. We were determined to dig that pearl out of the Sugar Maple.

We imagined the pearl was full of magic. We dreamed that it would make us rich. Oh, how our imaginations played tricks on us! Our mission was to dig that pearl out of the tree. Table knives, screwdrivers, ice picks, and nails were all used at one time or another in an effort to release the pearl. We dug until we had bulging blisters on our fingers, but the pearl was never meant to be ours.

Even after my grandparents sold that farm and moved, I always believed that I could hear that tree speaking to me, *"Come back, faithful one—come back to the secret place."* Beyond my childhood, I longed to go see the tree. The tree had encased secrets, laughter, and the innocence of a time long past. I tried to understand why God allowed me to have such vivid recollections of my time on that farm. Was it really just about the tree or was there more to it?

As I try to imagine myself back in the yard, I glimpse the silhouette of a child puttering around the kitchen with my grandmother. I look over my shoulder and watch the shadow of a child feeding horses through a barbed wire fence. I close my eyes and smell roses and daffodils. Fantasy melts into reality, and I finally have a clear revelation. The towering Sugar Maple was the center—the fortress, but it wasn't everything. Belief in a magical pearl kept me tied to the farm, but in the end, it wasn't what I cherished the very most in my heart. It was the entire place . . . the entire place that came to be known as my grandparents' farm.

CPSIA information can be obtained at www.ICGtesting.com
Printed in the USA
LVOW050305240712

291188LV00001B/5/P